REAL, RELEVANT, & Raw

Real Talk, Sacred Insight – You Asked, We Answered

Bishop James "Jai" Watson
Dr. Nikita "Ki" Garris-Watson

study, teaching, or devotional use, readers are encouraged to consult the full versions of each Bible translation.

Printed in the United States of America.

Book design by Dr. Ki Enterprises
Cover design by Dr. Ki Enterprises

ISBN - Paperback: 979-8-9897968-4-7
ISBN – E-book : 979-8-9897968-5-4

First Edition: April 2025

Preface: From Our Hearts to Yours

To every couple we've counseled, every individual who's asked, "Is love supposed to feel like this?", and every person wondering if strong relationships are still possible, we see you.

This book is not about us having all the answers. It's about what we've learned from **our mess, our ministry, and our marriage.** We've been married for 14 years. We're still growing, still laughing, still getting it wrong sometimes, and still choosing each other daily.

And in our role as faith leaders, we've sat in enough living rooms, prayer sessions, and counseling chairs to know this:
People don't need perfect examples. They need real encouragement, relatable wisdom, and hope that healing is possible.

This book is our offering.
Our stories.
Our truth.
Our love letter to the couples we've walked with, and the ones we've yet to meet.
We pray you'll see yourself in these pages.
And even more than that, we pray you'll see what's possible with honest communication, spiritual alignment, and a whole lot of grace.

Let's get into the real, the relevant, and yes, the raw.
With love,
+Bishop Jai & +Dr. Ki
(*Still married. Still learning. Still choosing love.*)

Table of Contents

Introduction: Real Talk Begins Here

So… why another relationship book?
Because let's be honest, love is beautiful, but it's also *messy*.
It's full of late-night talks, deep belly laughs, awkward apologies, silent treatments, passionate reconnections, and more "what did you just say?" moments than most folks care to admit.

We're not here as experts.
We're here as **witnesses**.

We've been married for almost 14 years. That's 168 months, 730 Sundays, and a whole lot of **grace, growth, and God** in between. Over those years, we've had front-row seats to each other's best and worst days. We've had the kind of love that makes you sing, and the kind of arguments that make you question your song selection.

As faith leaders who counsel couples and walk closely with those in every stage of love, dating, engaged, newly married, blended families, or hanging on by a thread, we noticed something consistent: **everyone has questions**. Real questions. Not the polished, filtered kind, but the kind you ask when no one else is around.

So, we decided to answer the top 25 relationship questions we've encountered along the way.

But not with fluff.
Not with formulas.
And definitely not with fairy tales.
We're giving you something **Real, Relevant, and Raw.**

Real:

Because we're sharing **our own stories**, the wins, the wounds, the lessons, and the laughter.

Relevant:
Because we speak to *what peoples are actually dealing with today*, communication breakdowns, sexual mismatches, parenting disagreements, emotional distance, money stress, and yes, even the healing after betrayal.

Raw:
Because you don't need a performance, you need permission to be honest, and a roadmap that's drenched in truth, grace, and wisdom from God's Word.

How to Use This Book

Welcome to a space where truth and tenderness meet, where hard questions aren't avoided, they're embraced with grace and answered with wisdom.

This book was born out of years of ministry, countless counseling sessions, and our own journey as a couple, learning, unlearning, falling, and getting back up with God's help. Every question in this book is real. Every response is rooted in experience. And every insight is prayerfully crafted with you in mind.

Here's what you can expect, and how to make the most of it:

1. Each Chapter Begins with a Real Question
We've taken the top 25 questions we've heard most often from individuals, married, engaged, dating, and single, and structured the book around them. These aren't surface questions. These are "if we don't deal with this, we won't make it" kind of questions.

2. You'll Read from Both of Us
Every answer includes a His Response (Bishop Jai) and a Her Response (Dr. Ki). Our answers are drawn from both our triumphs and our trials, because we believe testimony has power.

3. There's Room for God in Every Answer
This isn't just advice. It's biblical wisdom, wrapped in honesty and grace. Whether it's Scripture, prayer, or spiritual principle, you'll see God's heart woven through every answer.

4. Use the Reflections and Activities
Some chapters include additional checklists, prayer prompts, or activities to help you apply what you're reading. Don't skip them. These tools turn information into transformation.

You can read this book straight through, or go straight to the question that's hitting your heart right now. Either way, we encourage you to:

- Journal your reflections.
- Couples: Talk it out with your partner. Singles: Use it privately or invite an accountability partner along for the journey.
- Pray through the areas that challenge or inspire you.

5. This Book is for All Relationship Seasons

Whether you're:

- Married and want to grow or heal,
- Engaged and want to prepare,
- Dating and want to discern,
- Or single and want wisdom for the future,

There's something here for you. You don't have to have all the answers to start reading, you just have to be willing to grow.

Above all, we pray this book reminds you:
You're not alone.
Love can last.
And God is invested in your relationship more than you know.

Let's get real. Let's stay relevant. Let's go deep, and maybe even get a little raw.

Chapter One:

"CAN WE TALK ABOUT THIS?"

Question

How should communication and conflict be handled in a relationship?

Our Story

It started like many disagreements do: with assumptions and silence.

It was a typical Sunday afternoon. Church was great, worship was powerful, and the message really hit home, ironically, it was about "walking in love." We left hand in hand, spiritually full… and physically starving.

Now, we thought we had a plan. One of us (we won't say who) assumed we were eating leftovers at home. The other had been dreaming all morning of grabbing takeout on the way back. We pulled into the driveway, and I (the leftover planner) went straight for the kitchen. Meanwhile, my spouse was still in the car, looking confused, keys in hand like, "Aren't we going back out?"

Cue the tension.

What started as a minor miscommunication quickly escalated into frustration. One of us felt unheard. The other felt dismissed. The silence grew heavy. We ended up sitting on opposite sides of the couch, eating cereal, not because we didn't have food, but because the mood had shifted from sacred to sour.

Later that evening, after some space and a lot of internal processing, we did something that changed the trajectory of how we handle conflict now. We sat down and said four important words:

"So, what happened here?"

That simple question opened the door to honest dialogue. We realized we weren't mad about food, we were feeling disconnected, tired, and under-communicated. That moment taught us that conflict isn't always about the issue, it's about the unspoken things behind it.

He Says:

Listen, communication is not just about talking, it's about connecting. And let me tell you, there have been moments in our marriage when we were talking loudly but saying nothing.

I've learned that sometimes, I hear what my wife said, but not what she meant. And I've learned that when communication breaks down, conflict shows up with popcorn and a chair, ready to stay awhile.

Spiritually, James 1:19 lays it out:
"Be quick to listen, slow to speak, and slow to become angry."
That's divine advice for every man trying to lead with love and not ego.

Here's the practical side:

If you're always trying to be "right," you'll end up alone in your correctness.

If you interrupt her mid-sentence, you just volunteered for another hour of conflict.

And if you try to solve the issue without understanding it first… bro, don't do it. You're not the Holy Spirit.

Also: never underestimate the power of a snack. Most of our worst arguments could've been softened with some Chick-fil-A nuggets and a nap. I'm just saying, Jesus fed people before He preached.

The goal in conflict isn't to "win", it's to restore peace. It's to learn how to speak your truth without causing wounds. And to realize that sometimes the most powerful thing you can say is, "Help me understand where you're coming from."

That's kingdom communication. That's love.

She Says:

I used to think "good communication" just meant talking a lot, expressing every thought, every feeling, every opinion in the moment it came up. But over time, both through lived experience and the Spirit's guidance, I've learned that real communication is less about how much you say and more about *how deeply you connect.*
You can say all the right words and still miss the moment.
You can speak fluently and still fail to be understood.

For me, **communication is now about *intentional connection.***
It's about creating space for both of us to be heard, valued, and loved, even when we don't see things the same way.
Conflict is inevitable, especially when two different lives, stories, and personalities become one. But conflict doesn't have to be destructive. In fact, some of our greatest breakthroughs have come *after* disagreements, moments when we laid down our pride, took off the gloves, and chose humility over being "right."

One of the verses I carry close to my heart is **Proverbs 15:1**:
"A gentle answer turns away wrath, but a harsh word stirs up anger."
It reminds me that my delivery is just as important as my message. Words have weight, and tone has power. I don't want to just *say* something, I want to *build something* when I speak.

Here are a few things I've learned (sometimes the hard way) and now practice regularly:

1. Check My Tone.
The *what* may be right, but the *how* can still hurt.
I've asked the Lord to help me speak life, not just with truth, but with tenderness. Tone can open a heart, or shut it down completely.

2. Avoid Absolutes like "Never" and "Always."
These phrases don't invite understanding, they invite defensiveness. And when you put your partner on trial with your words, it's hard to build trust in the same breath.

3. Don't Fight to Be Right, Fight for the Relationship.
This one took me time to internalize. I've had to learn that "winning" the argument means nothing if it leaves the relationship wounded. The goal isn't to defeat my husband, it's to understand and grow *with* him.

4. Timing Is Everything.
I've learned to pause and ask, "Is this the right time for this conversation?"
Holy Spirit timing is just as important as Holy Spirit truth. Sometimes, the most loving thing you can do is wait until emotions settle, until you both can truly hear each other.

5. Check-In Before You Check-Out.
We've built a rhythm of regular check-ins, asking each other, "How are we really doing?" It's not deep every time. Sometimes we laugh, sometimes we cry, but we always come back to unity. Those moments help us stay ahead of misunderstandings before they grow into conflict.

And when tension *does* happen, and it will, we pray. Sometimes together, sometimes separately. But we always come back to the table with softened hearts and surrendered spirits. Our aim is never to "win" the fight. Our aim is to *win together.*

If you're in a relationship and struggling with communication, let me speak this over you: **You're not failing. You're learning.** Every couple grows at its own pace. There is no shame in struggling. What matters is that you stay committed, stay curious, and stay kind.

And sis, hear me clearly, **God can mature your mouth and anoint your ability to listen.** It's a process. One day at a time.

And if all else fails? Put the conversation on pause…
and go get ice cream. Because grace tastes better with caramel or sprinkles.

We Say:

Talk It Out, Don't Tear It Down: A Communication & Conflict Resolution Activity

Part 1: Communication Check-In (Self + Couple Assessment)
Rate the following statements on a scale from 1–5:
(1 = Never true | 3 = Sometimes true | 5 = Always true)

Individual Self-Reflection

☐ I actively listen without interrupting or forming a rebuttal in my head.

☐ I feel safe to speak honestly about my needs or concerns.

☐ I communicate in a respectful, calm tone even when frustrated.

☐ I recognize when I need a break or timeout from heated moments.

☐ I know how to ask for clarity or compromise without escalating tension.

Together as a Couple

☐ We listen to understand, not just to respond.

☐ We resolve disagreements in a way that brings peace, not prolonged silence.

☐ We avoid sarcasm, blame, and bringing up old issues during arguments.

☐ We schedule check-ins or quiet moments to talk through difficult topics.

☐ We invite God into our conversations before and after hard talks.

Part 2: "We Need to Talk" Ground Rules

Use these the next time a conflict arises, or to preempt one:

1. Set the Tone: Begin with prayer or silence to center yourselves.
2. Stick to the Topic: Focus on *one* issue at a time.
3. No Character Assassination: Address behavior, not identity (e.g., "What happened hurt me" vs. "You're selfish").
4. Active Listening: Repeat back what you heard before responding.
5. Permission to Pause: Either partner can request a timeout if overwhelmed, with a plan to return.
6. End with Intent: Ask, "What can we do better going forward?"

Build the Bridge Exercise (Together)

Each partner writes or shares:

- "One thing I appreciate about how you communicate is…"
- "One thing I would love us to improve is…"
- "When we argue, I feel ______ because ______."
- "The best way to help me feel heard is…"
- "Let's commit to one new communication habit this week: ______."

Couple's Prayer Prompt (For Conversation & Conflict)

"Lord, help us listen with our hearts, not just our ears. Give us patience when we disagree and grace when we fail. Teach us to speak truth with love and respond with wisdom. Heal any wounds caused by words. Help us grow not just in talking, but in understanding. Make our communication a source of connection, not division. In Jesus' name, amen."

Companion Scriptures for Communication & Conflict

- James 1:19 – "Everyone should be quick to listen, slow to speak and slow to become angry."
- Ephesians 4:29 – "Do not let any unwholesome talk come out of your mouths…"
- Proverbs 15:1 – "A gentle answer turns away wrath, but a harsh word stirs up anger."
- Colossians 4:6 – "Let your conversation be always full of grace…"

Chapter Two:

"STILL GOT THAT FIRE"

Question:

How can intimacy and passion be maintained over time?

Our Story

Let's just be honest, when we got married, we were already *grown grown*. We weren't newlyweds in our twenties discovering life together from scratch. We came into our marriage with high school-aged young people, ministry responsibilities, professional careers, and a combined collection of lived experience. So, when people ask us how we've kept the passion alive, we have to smile because for us, it wasn't about fighting for something we never had, it was about keeping sacred what we intentionally started.

Our reality wasn't diaper duty or newborn sleep deprivation, it was work responsibilities, senior projects, sports schedules, ministry prep, and making time for late-night conversations after showing up for our children and our ministry. And now that all of our children are adults, people assume keeping intimacy alive is easy, but here's the truth: **life doesn't slow down just because your kids grow up.**

Dr. Ki:
I remember one time we had plans to attend a jazz night, a rare treat. We had worked hard all week, scheduled everything around it, and then a church situation came up that required both of us. And just like that, the night we needed for *connection* became another night of *service*. And while we love what we do, we also had to learn that **intimacy suffers when everything else is allowed to come first**.

That's not selfish, that's stewardship. If we don't guard the space where we reconnect, resentment can creep in, and unmet emotional needs start looking like disinterest when really, it's just fatigue.

Bishop Jai:
That's why we had to grow. We had to stop overpromising ourselves to everyone else. We had to protect what we'd prayed for. There were

seasons we planned "just us" weekends around church events. Nights we ordered in, turned off the phones, and binge-watched shows that didn't even make sense, just to laugh and hold hands again. And yes, there were times when passion had to be *scheduled* like a business meeting. But it worked. Because we worked it.

He Says:

Let's keep it real, fellas, married passion isn't automatic. It's a ministry and a mystery. There's this myth that once you say, "I do," passion will just coast on autopilot for the next 50 years. Nah, bro. Passion takes participation.

We've been married long enough to know that the butterflies don't flutter on their own, you gotta keep feeding 'em. And it's not just about the bedroom (although that's part of it!). It's about the little things: those looks across the room, her favorite scent, doing the dishes without being asked (ladies, can I get an amen?).

From a spiritual perspective, Song of Solomon reminds us that passion is holy. God made it. He blessed it. And He didn't intend for it to burn out after year two. But here's the key, God never calls us to feel love all the time. He calls us to choose love. And choosing love means choosing intentionality.

Here's my advice: Keep dating her. Keep pursuing her. Keep laughing together, even when the jacuzzi is weird and the moment is off. Intimacy is built in the ordinary, not just the special occasions. Stay playful. Be spontaneous. And most importantly, invite God into even this part of your marriage.

Oh, and don't forget to pray before y'all plan a romantic weekend. Ask God to anoint the room, and the romance, He hears. you.

She Says:

It is often believed that passion is only about sparks, steamy moments, and heart-racing chemistry. And let's be clear, those things are wonderful. And yes, even after years of marriage, they're still necessary. *Romance is a gift from God, not a gimmick of the world.*
But the ultimate truth is that **true intimacy is much deeper than the physical, it's emotional, spiritual, and sacred.** It's a divine connection that invites both presence and purpose.

For my own marriage, it's the way he holds my hand when we pray and the way his voice softens when I've had a hard day.

It's how he helps me clean up after dinner, not because I asked, but because he wants to make room for us to sit, connect, and simply *be.*

It's the way he looks at me when I'm barefaced and in sweatpants and still says, "You're beautiful."

That's the kind of intimacy that lasts. It's not performative. It's *personal.*

God created intimacy to be **both physical and emotional**, not compartmentalized, but connected. And when we commit to nurturing *both*, passion doesn't disappear, it evolves. It grows up. It matures. It settles into something strong, rooted, and holy.

But like any garden, intimacy needs watering. It needs attention. It doesn't flourish on neglect or assumption. And it doesn't sustain itself on the memory of what once was. *It thrives in the intention of what still can be.*
Here are some valuable insights that I have gathered over time, personally and from walking with others:

1. Speak Up About Your Needs.

You cannot assume your spouse knows what you're feeling. God didn't design your partner to be a mind reader, He designed them to be a *listener.* Speak with clarity, not guilt. Share your desires without shame. And trust that healthy communication is not selfish, it's stewardship.

2. Flirt Often and Openly.

Yes, *flirt.* Send that text. Give that wink. Playfully interrupt him while he's shaving.

Romance doesn't have to be reserved for anniversaries. Keep the spark alive by intentionally tending to the fire, even if it's just a little at a time.

3. Stay Physically Engaged.

Intimacy isn't just about sex, it's about affection. A gentle touch, a soft kiss, a lingering hug. Those little moments build a bridge between hearts and bodies.

It's less about performance and more about connection.

4. Pray Together.

This may be the most powerful intimacy builder of all. When we pray together, we invite God into the space between us.

We anchor our hearts in His presence and open our spirits to hear beyond words. Spiritual intimacy is the soil where emotional and physical intimacy can grow.

One of my favorite verses is **1 Corinthians 13:7** –

"Love always protects, always trusts, always hopes, always perseveres."

That applies even in the seasons where passion feels low, or life feels heavy. **God gives us grace to persevere, and the creativity to rediscover each other again and again.**

To every wife reading this, and every woman preparing to be one:

- ✓ Never stop pursuing your husband, not just sexually, but emotionally, spiritually, and intentionally.
- ✓ Never stop praying for the fire to remain lit, even if it flickers.
- ✓ And never stop inviting God into the sacred space of your marriage.

Passion will shift in pace over time, but when love is rooted in **faith**, nurtured with **intention**, and stewarded with **grace**, it becomes more beautiful, more secure, and more fulfilling with every passing year.

Intimacy isn't just a moment, it's a ministry.
And with God in the center, it's one worth serving every single day.

We Say:

Keeping the Flame Alive: A Passion & Intimacy Check-In for Couples

Part 1: Where Are We Now? (Reflection Checklist)
Each partner answers honestly, individually or together:

Emotional Connection

- ☐ We have meaningful conversations beyond daily tasks.
- ☐ I feel emotionally safe and understood in our relationship.
- ☐ We regularly check in about how each other feels.

Physical Intimacy

- ☐ We express physical affection (kisses, cuddles, hugs) even outside the bedroom.
- ☐ We discuss our sexual needs, preferences, or desires with openness.
- ☐ We prioritize time for intimacy, not just when it's convenient.

Spiritual Unity

- ☐ We pray together about our relationship.
- ☐ We ask God to help us connect emotionally and physically.
- ☐ We invite God to heal any past wounds impacting our passion.

Part 2: Flame Finder Activity
Set aside 30–60 minutes for this connection activity (phones away, kids occupied, no distractions).

1. **Memory Lane Warm-Up**
   Each of you answer:

- What is one of your favorite intimate memories with me?
- When did you feel closest to me emotionally or physically?

2. **Five-Sense Spark**
   Each person chooses one way to reconnect through each sense:
   - Visual – Dress up for each other, send flirty notes, eye contact rituals
   - Auditory – Love playlist, affirming words, whisper prayers
   - Scent – Light candles, wear a favorite fragrance, shared bath time
   - Taste – Cook together, feed each other something sweet/spicy
   - Touch – Massage, hand-holding, cuddling with intention

3. **Passion Planner**
   Together, fill in these blanks:
   - A physical connection goal for this week: ______________
   - An emotional connection goal for this week: ____________
   - One intentional date or flirtation moment we'll plan this month: ____________

Spiritual Intimacy Moment (Couple's Prayer Prompt)

"God, help us love each other on purpose. Reignite our connection emotionally, spiritually, and physically. Let us see each other again with passion and patience. Help us remove distractions, break routines that divide us, and restore joy and playfulness in our relationship. We welcome laughter, affection, and creativity back into our love. In Jesus' name, amen."

Companion Scriptures for Intimacy Renewal

- **Song of Solomon 1:2** – "Let him kiss me with the kisses of his mouth…"
- **Proverbs 5:18–19** – "Rejoice in the wife of your youth…"
- **1 Corinthians 7:3–5** – "Do not deprive each other…"

Intimacy Readiness Check-In for Singles

"Before I give myself away, I make sure I know who I am."

Foundational Scripture:
Proverbs 4:23 (NLT) – *"Guard your heart above all else, for it determines the course of your life."*

Step 1: Self-Reflection – Where Am I?
Answer the following statements honestly, rating each from 1–5:
(1 = Not true at all, 5 = Very true)
Emotional Readiness

☐ I have dealt with past relationship wounds in a healthy, healing way.

☐ I do not carry resentment, unforgiveness, or bitterness from previous connections.

☐ I know how to express my needs without fear or guilt.

☐ I have healthy ways of handling conflict without withdrawing or exploding.

Spiritual Readiness

☐ I am committed to growing in my relationship with God, whether or not I'm in a relationship.

☐ I see singleness as a season of purpose, not punishment.

☐ I pray for God's will over my desire to be partnered.

☐ I trust God's timing more than my own.

Physical/Relational Awareness

☐ I understand my own physical boundaries and know how to communicate them.

☐ I value connection beyond physical attraction.

☐ I'm preparing for emotional and physical intimacy by investing in personal wholeness now.

☐ I'm willing to wait on the right connection rather than settle out of loneliness.

Total Score: _____ / 60

Reflection: What area is strongest? What area needs nurturing?

Step 2: Journal Prompt – "My Intimacy Inventory"

Reflect on the following in your journal:

1. What have I learned about intimacy from my past?
2. Where do I feel most confident in connection, and where do I feel afraid?
3. What habits, wounds, or beliefs do I need to surrender to God before inviting someone else in?
4. Am I prepared to give love the way I desire to receive it?

Step 3: Prayer of Preparation

Lord, prepare me for real love.

Help me to become emotionally whole, spiritually centered, and relationally wise.

Heal every place in me that still flinches from closeness. Break every agreement I've made with fear, shame, or isolation.

Teach me to guard my heart, not out of fear, but with wisdom.

And when the time comes, align me with someone who values intimacy the way You designed it, sacred, safe, and soul-deep.

Until then, be my wholeness.

Be my peace.

Be my portion.

In Jesus' name, amen.

Bonus Activity: "My Intimacy Affirmations"

Write and speak these aloud:

- I am whole with or without a relationship.
- I can express my needs without fear.
- I am worthy of love that sees me fully and handles me carefully.
- I am preparing for intimacy, not chasing it.
- I attract what I align with, peace, purpose, and purity.

Chapter Three:

"MORE THAN MONEY"

Question:

What are the best strategies for managing financial stress in a relationship?

Our Story:

Before we ever said, "I do," we both knew what it meant to struggle. We had each walked through seasons that humbled us, seasons where we faced financial lack, unexpected hardship, and yes, even homelessness. When we came together, we didn't bring lavish accounts or luxury lifestyles, we brought **faith, resilience, and a shared vow to honor God with whatever we had.**

We agreed early on that our marriage would be built on spiritual alignment, financial transparency, and faithful stewardship. We would tithe, *always*. We would talk, *regularly*. And we would trust God, *no matter what.*

But even with that agreement in place, we were not exempt from being tested.

Six months into our marriage, he lost his job.

No warning. No severance. Just a "thank you and goodbye." In that moment, every theory we had about trusting God turned into a lived reality. We were newly married, still adjusting to each other's rhythms, and now facing one of the most emotionally and financially destabilizing challenges a couple can face: the loss of income and the loss of identity that often comes with it.

And it wasn't the last time. Over the course of our marriage, we would face job loss again, and both times, **she** stepped into the role of sole provider. Not out of resentment. Not out of ego. But out of grace. Out of covenant.
But what made this even more layered was that our story didn't stop at the front door of our home.

We were, and still are, **pastors**.

Charged with leading a church. Teaching faith. Preaching provision. Pouring into others. And yet behind the scenes, we were making faith moves with grocery budgets and praying over the electric bill like it was revival night.

Add to that the financial strain of **college tuition**, supporting children through undergrad programs, supporting their dreams while stewarding our reality. There were months when we were balancing ministry, tuition payments, rent, and keeping the lights on in both our church and our home.

We don't share this for sympathy. We share this for someone who's there now, smiling on Sunday but crying in private. Leading with excellence but wondering, *"God, what about us?"*

And yet through every single season of strain, we saw the **faithfulness of God.**

We lost things but not our faith – we had a little faith on layaway for the hard times. We sowed. We served. We stayed. And God **provided**, sometimes in ways that didn't make sense, but always in ways that strengthened us.

Managing financial stress didn't start with numbers. It started with **agreement.**
With **grace.**
With **God.**

And from that place, we've grown stronger, not just as individuals, but as one.

He Says:

Let me tell you, nothing tests your faith in marriage like unexpected bills and a checking account that looks like it just went through a drought.

I'm a man who takes pride in taking care of home. Period. I've always believed it's my responsibility to provide, not just financially, but emotionally and spiritually too. So, when I lost my job six months into marriage, I felt like I lost my *footing* as a husband.

Now don't get me wrong, I never stopped praying, serving, or leading. But it's hard to feel like "the head" when your income just got cut off.

I'll never forget coming home and telling her. She didn't flinch. No meltdown. No judgment. Just a quiet, steady "We're going to be okay."

That right there? That was wealth. Because peace in the middle of pressure is priceless.

Financial stress will test your ego if you let it. But I had to learn this truth: **being a man isn't about how much you make, it's about how much you trust God when you can't make anything at all.** We didn't stop tithing. Didn't stop sowing. And somehow, God kept multiplying.

We had a few tense moments too. Like when she wanted to look over the budget *one more time*... or when I felt like I needed to "fix it" immediately. But we grew. I learned how to communicate better, how to receive support without feeling less than, and how to be covered *without crawling into a cave.*

My advice?

- **Pray more than you panic.**
- **Budget like you believe God honors stewardship.**
- **And don't confuse a season of lack with a lifetime of failure.**

Oh, and fellas? Let her help you if she can. It doesn't make you less of a man.
It makes you smart.

She Says:

Whew, financial stress? Been there. Budgeted that. Burned the receipts.

As someone who's worked in education, leadership, and administration, I've always believed in wise stewardship. I budget. I plan. I manage. I don't play when it comes to finances. But I also know what it's like to have degrees, discipline, and still not have enough.

That's why when I became the sole provider, not once but *twice*, I didn't see it as punishment. I saw it as **partnership.**

I didn't marry potential. I married purpose. And I knew our provision came from God, not just from a paycheck.

Were there stressful days? Of course.
Times when we had to say no to things we wanted. Times when I carried more and had to balance being a helpmate without becoming a martyr. But I stayed grounded in a few things:

- **We tithed no matter what.**
  Even when it didn't make "sense" on paper. Tithing wasn't optional, it was our covenant with the God who kept showing up.

- **We talked regularly about money.**
  No secrets. No silent resentment. We sat down, went over bills, and made plans together.

- **We leaned into grace.**
  There were moments when he felt the weight of "not providing." But I reminded him that *provision comes in many forms.* He prayed over us. Covered us. Protected our peace. That's provision, too.

For couples facing financial stress, my encouragement is this:

- ✓ Stay honest.
- ✓ Stay submitted to God.
- ✓ And stay off Instagram during your storm. (Comparison will make you question your process.)

And above all, **stay united**. It's not you versus your spouse. It's you *with* your spouse versus the challenge. So yes, money matters. But how you manage it together matters more. Teamwork, prayer, transparency, and a little humor can turn financial stress into financial strength.

We Say:

Faith & Finances: A Couple's Financial Stress Recovery Plan

Part 1: Financial Health Check-In (Couple Self-Assessment)
Together, rate each statement on a scale from 1 to 5:
(1 = Never True | 3 = Sometimes True | 5 = Always True)

Emotional Connection to Money

☐ We both feel comfortable talking about money without fear or shame.

☐ We are honest about our financial worries and expectations.

☐ We have grace for each other during seasons of financial difficulty.

Financial Management & Habits

☐ We know how much money is coming in and going out each month.

☐ We both participate in budgeting or financial decision-making.

☐ We set shared goals for saving, giving, or spending.

☐ We've adjusted our lifestyle when needed instead of blaming each other.

Spiritual Posture

☐ We pray together about our finances.

☐ We tithe or give consistently, even in small amounts.

☐ We trust God as our Source, not just our jobs or bank account.

Part 2: Financial Heart Talk (Couple Conversation Prompts)

Take turns responding to each prompt with vulnerability and grace:

1. "One thing I fear most about our finances is…"
2. "One thing I need from you when I'm financially stressed is…"
3. "When I feel financially insecure, I tend to…"
4. "One thing I appreciate about how we handle money is…"
5. "One change I think would help us move forward is…"

Part 3: Create a F.I.X. Plan (Faith, Insight, Execution)

F.I.X. Strategy	Action Step
Faith: How will we keep God at the center of our finances? (Prayer, giving, scripture study?)	______________________________
Insight: What financial truth or habit must we face honestly?	______________________________
Execution: What practical step can we take this week (budgeting, calling a creditor, adjusting spending)?	______________________________

Couple's Prayer Prompt: Prayer for Provision & Peace

"God, we thank You that You are Jehovah Jireh, our Provider. Even when money feels tight or uncertain, You have never failed us. Help us release fear, shame, and blame. Replace our anxiety with strategy. Teach us to be wise stewards, generous givers, and united in every financial decision. We trust You in lack and in overflow. Let peace rule in our home and provision flow through our hands. In Jesus' name, amen."

Scriptures for Financial Strength

- **Philippians 4:19** – "My God shall supply all your need…"
- **Proverbs 3:9–10** – "Honor the Lord with your wealth…"

- **Malachi 3:10** – "Bring the whole tithe… and see if I will not pour out a blessing…"
- **Matthew 6:33** – "Seek first His kingdom…"

Financial Preparedness Activity for Singles
"Wisdom is the foundation. Stewardship is the strategy."

Foundational Scripture:

Luke 14:28 (NLT) –

"But don't begin until you count the cost. For who would begin construction of a building without first calculating the cost to see if there is enough money to finish it?"

Part 1: Financial Heart Check – Reflect Before You Build

Answer the following questions honestly:

1. What was money like in the household I grew up in?
2. What emotions do I feel when I think about money (fear, anxiety, control, freedom, shame, excitement)?
3. Have I learned how to manage money biblically, or have I just been reacting to survival needs?
4. Do I believe God cares about my financial habits? Why or why not?

Part 2: Financial Health Self-Assessment

Rate yourself on a scale of 1–5 (1 = Not at all, 5 = Absolutely)

Statement	Rating
I consistently tithe or give intentionally from my income.	☐
I have a written monthly budget that I follow.	☐
I know exactly how much debt I have and have a plan to reduce it.	☐
I have savings or an emergency fund.	☐
I understand my financial triggers (emotional spending, guilt giving).	☐
I can discuss finances without feeling anxious or defensive.	☐
I have goals for financial growth (homeownership, giving, investing).	☐
I have financial boundaries when dating or in relationships.	☐

Total Score: _____ / 40
Reflection: Which area is strongest? Which needs the most growth?

Part 3: The "Before I Say I Do" Budget Blueprint

Take time to draft your current and desired monthly budget under the following categories:

Income

- Job(s): ___________
- Side hustles/gigs: ___________
- Other: ___________

Expenses

- Tithes & Offerings
- Rent/Mortgage
- Utilities
- Transportation
- Debt Repayment
- Groceries
- Savings
- Fun/Leisure
- Miscellaneous

Reflection Questions:

- Am I living within my means right now?
- If I were married tomorrow, what habits would help, or hurt, our financial stability?
- How am I preparing for shared financial responsibility?

Financial Alignment Prayer

Lord, make me a wise steward.

Teach me how to honor You with my finances, even in my single season.

Help me to release fear, develop discipline, and operate with integrity.

Break cycles of financial dysfunction and replace them with supernatural wisdom.

Prepare me now for the day I'll partner with someone else, so we can build together on a foundation of faith, order, and peace.

In Jesus' name, amen.

BONUS: Financial Boundaries for Dating

Write down your answers to these questions:

1. What financial boundaries do I need to set while dating?
2. How do I define generosity versus people-pleasing?
3. What red flags would concern me financially in a potential partner?
4. How do I plan to discuss finances early on in a relationship, with truth and grace?

Chapter Four:

"CALLINGS, CALENDARS & CUDDLES"

Question:

How do you balance careers, ministry, and personal lives?

Our Story

There was a season in our lives when our calendars were more anointed than our conversations. We were ministering everywhere, but connecting nowhere. We were both preaching three times a week, doing outreach in the community, and juggling demanding careers on top of it. Our phones buzzed with requests, prayer calls, and "Can you come speak at…" messages.

We were doing good things. God things. But somewhere in the middle of saying "yes" to everyone else, we started unintentionally saying "no" to each other.

One evening, we sat down, more roommates than spouses, each scrolling our own devices, when I quietly asked,
"When was the last time we laughed together?"

Silence.

That's when we knew something had to change. We didn't need another meeting. We needed margin. Not because we stopped loving each other, but because we needed to stop living like ministry partners and start acting like covenant partners again.

We had to revisit our original commitment when we decided to join in covenant: God is first. Our marriage second. Ministry and career flow from that, not over it.

He Says:

Let me keep it all the way real: you can be busy doing the Lord's work and forget to love like the Lord does at home.

There was a time when I was laying hands on folks at the altar, but giving short answers to my wife in the kitchen. I was working, pouring out sermons on Sunday, but had nothing left to give her by Friday. That's not balance, that's burnout with a holy soundtrack.

Here's what I've learned:

You can't minister effectively out there if you're falling apart in here.

The first ministry assignment God gave man was his home, not a platform.

I go back to 1 Peter 3:7 often:
"Husbands, live with your wives in an understanding way… so that your prayers may not be hindered."

In other words, fellas, God's not trying to hear your prayers or your sermons if you're ignoring your spouse.

Balance doesn't mean everything gets equal time, it means the right things get sacred time. So we:

Schedule regular date nights (yes, in the calendar like a staff meeting).

Set "no ministry talk" zones, sometimes the couch just needs to be for cuddles, not counseling strategy.

Have a Sabbath, even if it's a half day. We don't answer every call, and we don't feel guilty about it.

And listen, there's nothing more attractive than a wife who loves God and also wants to binge a show with you in lingerie or your t-shirt that she borrowed. That's holy ground too.

She Says:

When you're both in ministry and working careers, it can feel like you're giving your time, heart, and energy to everyone except each other.

I remember feeling so torn, between serving God, loving my husband, excelling at work, and still trying to find time for me. And I kept thinking, "Lord, if we're doing Your will, why does our relationship feel so depleted?"

That's when He reminded me:

"Your marriage is ministry. Rest is worship. Boundaries are holy."

Here's what helped us:

Prioritize your partnership. Ministry is beautiful, but marriage is sacred. We had to learn to protect our time together like we protect our prayer time and sermon prep. Intimacy and laughter matter just as much as strategy and service.

Share the load and the love. When one of us is overcommitted, the other gently helps reset. We've learned to check in with each other's bandwidth, not just schedules.

Create rhythms, not just routines. We built daily rhythms that help us stay connected, prayer walks, Kool-Aid talks, and even silent car rides where we just enjoy being together.

Don't compete, complement. We each have different callings and gifts, but we cheer each other on. I'm not intimidated by his calling, I'm inspired by it. And he covers mine in prayer and protection.

One verse that anchors me is Ecclesiastes 4:9–10:
"Two are better than one... If either of them falls down, one can help the other up."

Balancing it all isn't easy. But when we keep God at the center, protect our peace, and honor our marriage, we've found that we don't just survive ministry life, we thrive in it and through it.

For every couple juggling callings, careers, and each other: take a breath. Make time. Protect joy. And remember, your marriage doesn't compete with your ministry. It is your ministry.

We Say:

Blessed but Busy:
A Balance Check-In for Couples in Purpose and Partnership

Part 1: The Balance Audit (Reality Check + Reflection)
Rate the following areas individually, then discuss as a couple:
(1 = Never True | 3 = Sometimes | 5 = Always)

Spiritual & Personal Health

☐ I regularly spend quiet time with God outside of ministry obligations.

☐ I make time for personal rest, hobbies, or joy-inducing activities.

☐ I feel spiritually and emotionally refueled, not just poured out.

Marriage & Connection

☐ We prioritize each other outside of work and church functions.

☐ We schedule (not squeeze in) time together without distractions.

☐ We protect sacred space for emotional, physical, and spiritual intimacy.

Career & Ministry Balance

☐ We support each other's roles in both career and calling.

☐ We have clear expectations around ministry and job time.

☐ We discuss major decisions related to work or ministry together.

Boundaries & Burnout Prevention

☐ We recognize when we're overwhelmed and ask for help.

☐ We have healthy "no's" that protect our peace and priorities.

☐ We rest, not just crash, on a regular basis.

Part 2: The Sacred YES / Graced NO Activity

Step 1: Draw three circles on paper labeled:

- Circle 1: *What we must do (non-negotiable commitments)*
- Circle 2: *What we're called to do (assignments for the season)*
- Circle 3: *What we feel pressured to do (that may need to go)*

Step 2: As a couple, write tasks, roles, or expectations into the appropriate circle.

Step 3: Decide together:

- What can be delegated?
- What needs to be put on pause?
- What deserves a renewed "yes"?
- Where is God asking for margin, not more movement?

Part 3: Rhythm Reset & Realignment Plan

Area	Rhythm or Boundary to Protect	When It Happens	Who Holds It Accountable
Time with God (individually)	____________	________	________
Time with Each Other	____________	________	________
Rest/Sabbath	____________	________	________
Ministry Work	____________	________	________

Area	Rhythm or Boundary to Protect	When It Happens	Who Holds It Accountable
Career/Work Focus	___________________	__________	__________

Tip: Start with what you can consistently maintain, not just what sounds ideal.

Couple's Prayer Prompt: For Rhythm, Rest & Refocus

"God, we thank You for every assignment You've given us, at work, in ministry, and in our marriage. Help us not lose each other while doing good things. Give us wisdom to manage time, energy, and emotions. Teach us how to rest, how to reconnect, and how to say 'no' without guilt. Help us steward this life well, together and with joy. In Jesus' name, amen."

Scriptures for Wisdom & Balance

- **Ecclesiastes 3:1** – "There is a time for everything…"
- **Matthew 11:28** – "Come to me… and I will give you rest."
- **Proverbs 16:3** – "Commit your plans to the Lord…"
- **Mark 6:31** – "Come with me… and get some rest."

Chapter Five:

"GREEN EYES, GENTLE HEARTS"

Question:

What are healthy ways to deal with jealousy and insecurity in a relationship?

Our Story:

We were about two years into marriage when the green-eyed monster showed up, quietly, subtly, and completely uninvited.

It started with little things. A lingering glance someone gave him at church. The compliments she got from a coworker. A social media message that didn't sit quite right. Nothing dramatic, just enough to stir questions like, "Am I enough?" or "Does he notice her?" or "Why is she complimenting him like that?"

One day, after an event, someone thrust herself between me and my husband, demanding his attention, and something in me flared. I smiled politely, but when we got in the car, I said, "You didn't see her disrespect me?"

He blinked. "Wait…what just happened?"

What happened was disrespectful, but it was also insecurity I hadn't even fully acknowledged, rooted not in him, but in me.

That moment led to one of our most vulnerable and healing conversations. We realized jealousy wasn't always about what the other person was doing, it was often about what we believed (or didn't believe) about ourselves. And healing that required truth, trust, and grace.

He Says:

Let me be honest, jealousy and insecurity are sneaky. They don't kick down the door yelling, "I'm here!" They slide in with suspicion, side-eyes, and internal questions like, "Why'd she like that post?" or "You've never said I look like that…"

But I've learned that jealousy isn't really about her actions, it's about my identity.

As a man, there were times I wrestled with insecurity too. If someone made my wife laugh a little too hard or complimented her leadership, I'd smile on the outside and wonder, "Am I doing enough?" But here's the truth: insecurity grows in silence. It shrinks in transparency.

Here's what's helped me:

Speak what's real before it becomes resentment. If something's bothering you, say it with honesty, not hostility.

Reaffirm your partner. Compliment her. Notice her. Celebrate her. Insecurity fades when love is loud and consistent.

I go back to **Psalm 139** often: *"I am fearfully and wonderfully made."* That includes my role as a husband. I'm not perfect, but I'm chosen, and that truth silences every whisper of inadequacy.

I remind myself daily that God didn't just call me to be a husband, He's equipping me to be the *best possible* husband for **her**. That means being present, being teachable, and being prayerful. It means leading with love, serving with humility, and growing with grace. I may not always get it right, but I show up with a willing heart and a surrendered spirit, because who I am in Christ gives me the courage to become everything, she needs in me.

Also, pro tip: if she's feeling insecure, don't say, "You're overthinking it." That's a fast track to an emotional shutdown. Say, "Help me understand what you're feeling." It's not about fixing, it's about feeling with.

And if jealousy ever tries to creep in, remind yourself: comparison is a thief, but communication is a builder.

She Says:

Whew, jealousy and insecurity? Yes, sis… I've been there. And not just once.

It's easy to assume that once you're married, those feelings disappear. But the truth is, even in a healthy, God-honoring relationship, insecurity can show up in whispers like:

"What if they think she's prettier than me?"

"He's succeeding and I'm struggling, what if he outgrows me?"

"I don't look like I did five years ago, what if he notices?"

First, let's normalize this: You're not weak for having moments of insecurity. You're human.

The truth:

Jealousy is a natural emotion that often arises when we compare ourselves to others. In today's digital age, social media amplifies this tendency, showcasing curated lives that can make us feel inadequate. Past wounds and unspoken expectations further fuel this fire, creating a cycle of envy and discontent. The antidote to this destructive pattern is real, honest, face-to-face connection. When we take the time to truly connect with others, we move beyond superficial comparisons and foster genuine relationships. These connections remind us of our shared humanity and help us appreciate our unique journeys. By prioritizing authentic interactions, we can break free from the grip of jealousy and cultivate a sense of belonging and peace.

Insecurity is a deeply rooted issue that thrives in the shadows of our minds. To heal, it requires exposure to the light of truth and love. Confessing our fears to God and to trusted individuals, like a spouse, is a powerful step towards healing. This confession is not about shame, but about surrendering our burdens and seeking support.

When we open up about our insecurities, we invite healing into our lives. God's grace and the understanding of loved ones can provide the comfort and strength needed to overcome these fears. By embracing vulnerability and seeking help, we can transform insecurity into a source of growth and resilience. This journey of healing is marked by spiritual strength, kindness, and the wisdom of an expert guiding us towards wholeness.

Speak life over yourself. Proverbs 18:21 says, “Death and life are in the power of the tongue.” I started declaring truth: “I am loved. I am seen. I am secure in God, and in this marriage.”

And my husband? He became my partner in building confidence, not because it was his job to “fix” me, but because we chose to be safe spaces for one another.

Sister Friends, if you’re struggling with jealousy or insecurity, know this: you are not alone, and you are not broken. Bring your feelings into the light. Let God and your spouse love you through them. Real security doesn’t come from control, it comes from covenant.

Let love speak louder than fear.

We Say:

Secure Love: A Jealousy & Insecurity Healing Activity

Part 1: Insecurity Inventory (Self-Reflection Checklist)
Each partner answers individually:

☐ I am aware of the specific areas where I feel insecure or not enough.

☐ I can identify whether my insecurity is rooted in past trauma or current behavior.

☐ I have clearly expressed my insecurities to my partner without blame or shame.

☐ I believe I am worthy of love, even when I feel vulnerable.

☐ I feel secure in this relationship most of the time.

☐ I can celebrate my partner's strengths without questioning my own value.

☐ I take responsibility for managing my internal fears and triggers.

Part 2: Reassurance Repair Plan (As a Couple)
Take turns responding to these prompts:

1. **"When I feel jealous or insecure, I usually… "**
2. **"The most reassuring thing you've done or said was… "**
3. **"I need you to remember that I feel safe when… "**
4. **"A trigger I didn't realize was impacting me is… "**
5. **"Together, I want us to grow in emotional security by… "**

Then, work together to complete the following **Security Pact:**

Security Practice	What We'll Do Together
Speak truth in love when insecurities arise	____________________________

Security Practice	What We'll Do Together
Avoid comparison and competition	______________________
Affirm each other's worth verbally and often	______________________
Pray over identity, value, and trust	______________________
Practice grace when one of us is triggered	______________________

Truth Over Trigger Affirmation Exercise

Together, choose 3 affirmations you'll speak over each other when jealousy or insecurity creeps in:

- "I choose to trust you and not fear what hasn't happened."
- "You are enough, and you are loved as you are."
- "God is still healing us both, and I'm staying through the process."

You can also write your own:

-
-
-

Couple's Prayer Prompt: For Security, Healing & Clarity

"God, we come against every lie that has made us feel unworthy, unseen, or unsafe. We break the spirit of jealousy and insecurity. Heal every old wound that's creating new tension. Let us build trust, give affirmation, and walk in emotional and spiritual confidence. Remind us that love doesn't compete, it covers, believes, and protects. In Jesus' name, amen."

Scriptures for Insecurity & Jealousy

- **Psalm 139:14** – "I praise you because I am fearfully and wonderfully made."
- **1 Corinthians 13:4–5** – "Love is patient… it does not envy…"

- **Isaiah 41:10** – "Do not fear, for I am with you…"
- **James 3:16** – "For where you have envy… there you find disorder…"

Insecurity & Jealousy Checklist for Singles

"Before I share my heart, I ask God to search it."

Foundational Scripture:

Psalm 139:23–24 (NIV)

"Search me, God, and know my heart; test me and know my anxious thoughts. See if there is any offensive way in me, and lead me in the way everlasting."

Self-Check: Answer Yes or No Honestly

Statement	Yes	No
I sometimes compare myself to others in relationships or on social media.	☐	☐
I worry that I'm not "enough" emotionally, spiritually, or physically for a future partner.	☐	☐
I've experienced jealousy in past relationships and didn't fully resolve it.	☐	☐
When someone I'm interested in talks to others, I feel threatened or anxious.	☐	☐
I often need external validation to feel confident.	☐	☐
I've been hurt before and still fear being replaced, rejected, or abandoned.	☐	☐
I sometimes feel the need to "prove" my worth in order to be loved or chosen.	☐	☐
When I see others in relationships, I sometimes feel overlooked or less than.	☐	☐
I secretly compare my timeline to others and feel behind in life or love.	☐	☐
I trust God in many areas, but struggle to fully trust Him with my love life.	☐	☐

Reflection: If you answered "yes" to **4 or more**, it's time to pause and invite the Holy Spirit into those places. These aren't flaws, they're flags calling for healing.

Journal Prompts: Invite God into the Process

1. Where did my insecurities begin? Are they tied to past relationships, family dynamics, or inner dialogue?
2. How do jealousy and comparison show up in my life, subtly or loudly?
3. What truths does God speak over me that I sometimes forget?
4. What kind of partner do I want to be, and what kind of heart do I want to bring into a relationship?
5. Who or what do I need to forgive (including myself) to move forward in freedom?

Prayer of Release & Restoration

Father, heal the hidden places.

I bring You every wound, every word, and every fear that has shaped how I see myself.

Uproot insecurity and replace it with identity.

Uproot jealousy and replace it with joy.

Teach me to trust, not just others, but You, completely.

Prepare my heart to love from wholeness, not from hurt.

And when the time comes to share my life with someone, let it be from a place of confidence, peace, and spiritual clarity.

In Jesus' name, amen.

Speak Life: Insecurity-Fighting Affirmations

- I am whole in God before I am ever partnered with anyone.
- I am not in competition with anyone, I am in covenant with God.
- I am worthy of love that doesn't require proving.
- I celebrate others without comparing my journey.
- God's timing is perfect. I lack nothing.

Chapter Six:

"BUILT TO LAST"

Question:

What are the keys to a long-term relationship?

Our Story:

We once had someone ask us at a retreat, "How have you stayed together?" and before either of us could answer, one of us jokingly said, "Short memory and strong prayer life!"

And while we laughed, there was more truth in that than we initially realized.

Long-term love isn't built on perfect days. It's built on purposeful days.

We've weathered life's seasons, job changes, ministry burnout, grief, parenting, financial dips, misunderstandings, and moments when the only thing holding us together was the promise we made before God.

There were times we didn't feel in love, but we always chose love.

Over time, we realized that staying together doesn't happen by default, it happens by design. We learned to build rhythms, not just routines. To give grace, not just gifts. And to prioritize we over me.

Our relationship didn't just survive because we were "compatible." It lasted because we committed to grow, together.

He Says:

Let's be real, anybody can be in love for a season. But it takes God, grit, and grace to be in love for a lifetime.

When folks ask me the secret to staying married, I give them three words:
Work. Prayer. Laughter.

Because truthfully:

You won't always like each other, but you're still called to love each other.

You won't always agree, but you can always choose peace over pride.

And some days, the best marriage ministry is a shared bowl of popcorn and a comedy movie.

From a spiritual standpoint, I cling to Ecclesiastes 4:12:
"Though one may be overpowered, two can defend themselves. A cord of three strands is not quickly broken."

That third strand? That's God. He's the glue. The guide. The grace-giver.

Here's what I've learned as a husband:

Be consistent, not just passionate. Love isn't proven in big moments, it's built in daily faithfulness.

Stay curious about your spouse. The moment you think you've "figured them out," you stop pursuing them. Keep asking questions. Keep learning them.

Forgive fast. There's no scoreboard in marriage. Either you both win, or nobody does.

And my last tip? Don't just grow old together, grow up together. Mature love isn't afraid to say, "I was wrong." Or, "Let's try again." Or, "Pass me the remote and come cuddle."

She Says:

Intentionality is the cornerstone of our enduring relationship. Through every high and low, it has been our deliberate actions and choices that have strengthened our bond. Intentionality means making a conscious effort to prioritize each other, to communicate openly, and to nurture our connection. It involves setting aside time for meaningful conversations, showing appreciation, and supporting each other's dreams and aspirations. By being intentional, we create a safe space where love can flourish, even in the face of challenges.

This purposeful approach to our relationship has been the guiding light that has kept us together, reminding us that love is not just a feeling, but a series of intentional acts that build a strong and lasting foundation.

Long-term love is a journey that requires dedication and effort. It is not something that magically appears; it is a choice we make every day. Choosing to love means committing to each other, even when times are tough. It involves cultivating our relationship through acts of kindness, patience, and understanding. We must be willing to invest time and energy into nurturing our love, just as we would tend to a garden. This cultivation process is enriched by grace, which allows us to forgive, to be compassionate, and to grow together.

Grace covers our imperfections and helps us navigate the complexities of life with a spirit of humility and gratitude. By choosing, cultivating, and embracing grace, we create a love that is resilient, enduring, and deeply fulfilling.
Here's what's been key for me as a wife:

Keep God first, always. When I'm grounded in Him, I'm more patient, more forgiving, and more able to see my husband through His eyes, not just mine.

Protect your connection. Whether it's 15 minutes of uninterrupted talk time or praying together before bed, little things keep your hearts tied together.

Stay friends. Yes, lovers. Yes, partners. But friendship is what keeps it light, fun, and real. Laugh often. Tease kindly. Flirt with each other, even after 5, 10, 20, 30 years.

One verse that has shaped my view of lasting love is 1 Corinthians 13:7 –
"Love bears all things, believes all things, hopes all things, endures all things."

Enduring love isn't heavy when it's built on hope and filled with laughter.

Also, let's normalize that long-term love doesn't mean a conflict-free life. We've had hard seasons. But those seasons taught us how to fight fair, pray hard, and stay humble.

You don't build a long-term relationship by avoiding storms, you build it by learning to dance (and sometimes cry) in the rain.

Here's our encouragement to you: Keep showing up. Keep choosing grace. Keep inviting God into the middle. That's how love lasts, not because it's flawless, but because it's faithful.

We Say:

Built to Last: A Longevity & Legacy Activity for Lasting Love

Part 1: Longevity Check-Up (Self & Couple Reflection)
Each partner answers honestly. Rate on a scale from 1–5:
(1 = Never true | 3 = Sometimes true | 5 = Consistently true)

Spiritual & Emotional Foundation

☐ We pray together consistently.

☐ We forgive each other quickly and sincerely.

☐ We prioritize our spiritual growth as individuals and as a couple.

☐ We work through conflict without tearing down character.

Connection & Commitment

☐ We enjoy being around each other, even in silence.

☐ We have shared values, goals, or vision for the future.

☐ We revisit our relationship purpose often.

☐ We show up for each other even when we don't feel emotionally full.

Growth & Grace

☐ We give each other space to grow without judgment.

☐ We celebrate small wins in our relationship.

☐ We address hard issues instead of ignoring them.

☐ We actively invest in improving our relationship.

Part 2: The Legacy Map (Long-Term Visioning Activity)
Complete this together as a couple:

Our Relationship Was Planted On…
(What foundational values or principles brought us together?)
→ ____

Our Relationship Is Currently Growing In…
(Where are we learning, stretching, or maturing?)
→ ____

Our Relationship Will Bear Fruit In…
(What impact do we want our love to have on others, children, community, friends?)
→ ____

What Threatens Our Long-Term Connection?
(List 1–2 consistent stressors, bad habits, or unresolved patterns.)
→ ____

What Protects Our Love & Future?
(Spiritual disciplines, rituals, friends, therapy, etc.)
→ ____

Commitment Check-In Questions (Quarterly or Annually)
Discuss the following:

1. "What's one thing I've done this year that made you feel secure in our relationship?"
2. "What's one area we could be more intentional about investing in?"
3. "Are there any wounds, assumptions, or fears we've ignored too long?"
4. "What's our next shared milestone or memory we want to create together?"
5. "What legacy do we want to leave through our love?"

Couple's Prayer Prompt: For Endurance, Joy, and Legacy
"God, thank You for giving us each other, not just for the good days, but for the growth days. Strengthen our roots. Stretch our love. Make us unshakable through storms, unoffendable in conflict, and

unmovable in faith. Help us live out a love that reflects You, faithful, forgiving, and full of joy. Let our relationship bear good fruit for years to come. In Jesus' name, amen."

Scriptures for Long-Term Love & Commitment

- **1 Corinthians 13:7** – "Love always protects, always trusts, always hopes, always perseveres."
- **Ecclesiastes 4:12** – "A cord of three strands is not quickly broken."
- **Galatians 6:9** – "Let us not become weary in doing good…"
- **Proverbs 24:3–4** – "By wisdom a house is built…"

Are You Built for Longevity?

A Heart & Mind Readiness Assessment for Singles

"Because lasting love begins with lasting wholeness."

Foundational Scripture:

Luke 6:48 (NIV) –

"They are like a man building a house, who dug down deep and laid the foundation on rock. When a flood came, the torrent struck that house but could not shake it, because it was well built."

Longevity Readiness Checklist

Statement	**Yes**	**No**
I have dealt with (or am actively healing from) past relationship pain or trauma.	☐	☐
I can resolve conflict with maturity, prayer, and communication, not just silence or anger.	☐	☐
I understand that real love involves both sacrifice and support.	☐	☐
I have a consistent relationship with God and seek His guidance before entering partnerships.	☐	☐
I can listen, even when I don't agree, without attacking or shutting down.	☐	☐
I see love as a daily choice, not just a fleeting feeling.	☐	☐
I'm not afraid of accountability in a relationship.	☐	☐
I'm emotionally available and capable of showing affection and vulnerability.	☐	☐
I have financial, spiritual, and emotional goals that align with healthy partnership.	☐	☐
I understand that submission and leadership in love are about mutual trust and honor.	☐	☐
I'm willing to forgive, communicate, and grow, *even when it's hard.*	☐	☐
I have boundaries that protect peace, not build walls.	☐	☐

Reflection:

- **10–12 Yes answers**: You're grounded and God-aligned, ready for something lasting.
- **6–9 Yes answers**: You're growing and gaining awareness, keep building.
- **0–5 Yes answers**: Start by going deeper with God and healing your foundation first.

Journaling Prompts:

- What does *longevity* in love mean to me, and how has God redefined it?
- What patterns have I repeated that I want to break?
- In what ways have I prepared myself to *be* a promise, not just pray for one?
- Who am I becoming when no one is watching, and how does that affect what I'll build?

Prayer for Longevity Readiness

Lord, prepare me for something that lasts.

Before I commit to someone else, help me commit fully to You.
Build my foundation on truth, wisdom, and grace.
Heal every part of me that isn't ready to sustain love.
Give me the patience to grow, the strength to let go of what won't last,
and the clarity to recognize what You've designed for me.
I want love that lasts, and I trust You to lead me there.
In Jesus' name, amen.

Longevity Mindset Affirmations

- I am not rushing, I am *rooting*.
- I am built for covenant, not chaos.
- I bring healing, not harm.
- I'm preparing for something that can weather storms.
- I trust God's timing because I trust God's love for me.

Chapter Seven:

"WHAT DO YOU NEED FROM ME?"

Question:

How can we better understand each other's needs?

Our Story:

Our dynamic is different from the norm.

A lot of couples have a wife who's expressive and emotionally in tune, and a husband who wants to swoop in and fix things. In our marriage? It's flipped.

I (Bishop Jai) often don't know how to identify what I'm feeling, much less what I need. I've spent years being the calm, steady one, the "I'm good" guy. Meanwhile, my wife? She's intuitive, detailed, and solution-oriented. The moment she sees a crack, she's got blueprints, tools, and a ten-step action plan.

One evening, after a long week where I was emotionally distant and mentally drained, she sat me down, concern written all over her face. She said, "What's going on with you? You've been off."

I sighed, rubbed the back of my neck, and said honestly, "I don't even know."

That's when we both realized, understanding each other's needs wasn't just about asking the right questions, but about creating space for the answers to emerge… even if they came slowly, gently, or wordlessly.

He Says:

Let me say this upfront: I don't always know what I need.

I know when I'm overwhelmed. I know when I feel numb. I know when I get quiet and disappear into tasks, routines, or distractions. But if you were to ask, "What do you need right now?" my answer is often, "I'm not sure."

That used to frustrate my wife. Not because she lacked patience, but because she genuinely wanted to help. She wanted to fix, offer solutions, bring me peace. But I didn't know what to hand her.

Here's what I've learned:

Silence doesn't always mean peace. Sometimes, silence means I'm sorting through things I don't have language for yet.

I have to be intentional about self-awareness. If I don't take time to reflect, rest, and check in with myself and with God, I'll drift into emotional autopilot, and that's not fair to either of us.

God gives insight when we ask. I've started praying Psalm 139:23–24: "Search me, O God, and know my heart… See if there is any offensive way in me, and lead me in the way everlasting." Sometimes understanding my needs starts with letting the Holy Spirit shine a light on what's going on beneath the surface.

And to the men reading this: It's okay not to have all the answers. What matters is that we're willing to slow down, tune in, and try. That we invite our wives into the process, not just for solutions, but for support.

Because sometimes what we need most is to know we're safe to say, "I'm not okay right now," and not be rushed to get better, but loved while we're figuring it out.

She Says:

I'll admit, I'm the fixer.

As an ISTJ, I live by structure, order, and solutions. If there's a problem, I want to fix it. Not tomorrow. Not eventually. But *now*. I'm not one for long speeches or emotional guessing games, I listen for the problem, I identify the pattern, and I get to work.

If there's tension, I want a resolution. If I see pain, I want to bring healing. If my husband's off, I want to ask a hundred questions until he "gets better." That's how I'm wired. That's how I love.

But I had to learn the hard (and holy) way: being a good partner doesn't always mean fixing the problem, it means being present through the process. I had to face a fact that wasn't in any of my planners or spreadsheets: **I can't fix what hasn't been named.**

And my husband, bless his adventurous, expressive, spontaneous heart, *didn't always know how to name it.*

As an ESFP-T, he feels deeply, loves hard, and brings life to every room he enters. But when it comes to **his own needs**, he often wrestles in silence. Not because he's hiding, but because he's still figuring them out. He'll make everyone laugh, make sure I'm okay, and keep life light, but there were moments I'd look at him and *know* something was off… even when he didn't have the words to say it.

That was hard for me.
I wanted to help. To plan. To fix.
But sometimes my *fixing* looked like frustration.
And his *silence* looked like avoidance.
And we both ended up feeling unheard.

Early in our marriage, I'd push.
"Talk to me. What's wrong? Just tell me what you need!"
But one day, I heard God whisper, "He doesn't need a solution, he needs safety."

That shifted everything. I came to recognize that **understanding your spouse's needs isn't always about solving, it's about slowing down long enough to listen between the lines.**

Now, instead of interrogating, I ask, "How can I support you today?" or "Do you need space, or do you want company?" Sometimes I get an answer. Sometimes I just sit next to him while we say nothing at all. And both are sacred.

I resist the urge to jump in with a solution. This was the hardest for me. I had to remind myself: my job is to *be present*, not be perfect. Sometimes he just needs a safe space to feel, not a step-by-step plan to fix it.

I study his rhythms, not just his words. There were days I could sense when he needed encouragement, even if he never said it. I've learned to lean into his energy. If the life-of-the-party seems quiet or disconnected, it's a cue, not a character change.

When I'm tempted to press for answers, I've learned to pray for clarity. God sees the places in my husband that he doesn't always know how to articulate, and when I surrender my need to *know*, God helps me to love him through it. This has taught me to **pray more than I push.**

One scripture that changed my approach is Galatians 6:2:
"Carry each other's burdens, and in this way, you will fulfill the law of Christ."

That doesn't mean I carry them for him – although I would willingly do so. Instead, I walk with him, offering patience, peace, and presence.

And while I'm still a fixer at heart, I've grown into something deeper: **a better listener. A partner. A student of the man I love.** Because sometimes the greatest gift isn't fixing the problem, it's *faithfully walking with him until he can name it for himself.*

So to the women like me, with hearts that want to help and hands that want to fix:

Remember, your love is most powerful when it's gentle. When it waits, listens, and wraps him in grace while he finds the words for what he needs.

Sometimes, our husbands don't need us to lead them to a solution. They just need us to be the safe place they can land while they learn to name their own needs.

We Say:

Understanding and Responding to Each Other's Needs

Scripture Anchor:
"Each of you should look not only to your own interests, but also to the interests of others." Philippians 2:4 (NIV)

Start With Prayer (Together):
"Lord, help us to speak from a place of truth and hear from a place of love. Teach us to express our needs without fear and respond to one another without judgment. Give us the grace to care for each other's hearts like You care for ours. Amen."

Step 1: Self-Reflection (Individually)
Take 5–10 minutes in silence. Reflect on what you currently need in the relationship, emotionally, spiritually, and physically. Then, complete the following prompt privately:

"Right now, I need…"

Type of Need	**Your Response**
Emotional	(e.g. more quality time, affirmation, empathy)
Physical	(e.g. rest, affection, intimacy, help around the house)
Spiritual	(e.g. prayer, devotional time together, encouragement)
Practical	(e.g. support with a project, financial planning)

Step 2: Share Gently With Each Other
Each partner reads their list out loud, without interruption.

The listener uses these 3 phrases:
"Thank you for sharing that with me."

"I didn't realize that was so important to you, thank you for helping me understand."

"How can I practically support that need this week?"

Step 3: Write a "Needs-in-Action" Plan
Together, choose 1–2 needs per person to focus on this week.

	Partner Need	Support Action This Week
Partner A	______________	______________________
Partner B	______________	______________________

Step 4: Check Back In
Schedule a follow-up check-in in 3–7 days. **Ask:**
"Did I meet the need the way you hoped?"
"Did I misunderstand or overlook anything?"
"What did this experience teach us about each other?"

Bonus Tips:
Don't wait until you're frustrated to check in, make it a regular rhythm.
Remember: needs aren't demands, they're invitations to love better.
Affirm progress. Even small steps deserve celebration.

Closing Scripture to Reflect On:
"Carry each other's burdens, and in this way you will fulfill the law of Christ." Galatians 6:2

Closing Prayer (Together):
"God, thank You for reminding us that our needs matter, and so do our spouse's. Help us love without assumptions, speak without fear, and serve one another with joy. Make our marriage a safe place for honesty, healing, and growth. In Jesus' name, amen."

Chapter Eight:

"LETTING GO WHILE STAYING CLOSE"

Question:

What are effective ways to deal with differences in parenting styles?

Our Story:

When we got married, we brought more than vows, we brought **teenagers, college-aged kids, and the layered beauty of a blended family**. We also brought two different parenting backgrounds, a few parenting scars, and one clear shared value: *"Kids need structure."*

We both believed in consistency, accountability, and intentional parenting. We were united on what we believed, *but life didn't always give us control over how it played out.*

At the time, my daughter lived with us, my son lived between us and my ex-husband, and his children lived with his ex-wife. So even though we were married and spiritually aligned, **we were parenting in three different households**, with two other adults who didn't necessarily share our same philosophy or approach.

And then came the young adult years.
Gone were the days of curfews and consequences. These weren't toddlers asking for juice boxes, they were nearly grown, forming opinions, facing real-world choices, and wrestling with independence. And the hardest part? We weren't always the voice they listened to. Sometimes, we weren't even the voice they heard.

There were moments when it felt like we were **building fences**, trying to offer structure and wisdom, while the other households were **throwing open gates**, saying, "They'll figure it out," or "Let them be."

And we felt it.

We felt like the *strict ones*. The *too involved ones*. The *overbearing ones*. There were holidays we cried behind closed doors. Phone calls that left us questioning everything. Decisions made without our input. And situations where our standards felt not just ignored, but undermined.

But God.

Through late-night conversations, sometimes filled with laughter, sometimes with frustration, and through many *tear-stained, wisdom-seeking prayers*, we came to understand a powerful truth:
Parenting young adults isn't about control. It's about connection.

They don't just need our protection. They need our presence.
We had to release the myth of being the "perfect parents" and embrace the grace of being *present ones*, those who stand in love, offer wisdom, and *trust God with what we can't control.*
We learned to:

- **Pray instead of pressure.**
- **Cover them, even when we couldn't correct them.**
- **Stay unified as a couple, even when navigating with former spouses.**

It hasn't always been easy. There are still moments when our hearts break quietly or when we disagree on just how much room to give. But what's kept us grounded is knowing that love isn't measured by control, it's measured by consistency, even when you're not in the driver's seat.

And in this blended, beautiful, sometimes chaotic family?
Love wins. Grace covers. And presence matters.

He Says:

Structure Was My Love Language… Until It Wasn't Listen, I was raised to believe structure *is* love.

Chores. Curfews. Respect. Consequences. That's how you raise solid people, right? I didn't grow up with a lot of softness, but I had order, and that kept me focused.

So when we got married and stepped into a blended family with young adults already on their own timelines, it was a culture shock.

My kids, her kids, our exes. That meant three different households, three different styles, and three different sets of "house rules."
And suddenly, *structure* started to look more like *tension.* There were no stepchildren; we don't use that term - they are our children - but there was stress.

We'd try to enforce standards, and they'd push back, or worse, pull away.

When they missed deadlines, made impulsive decisions, or ignored guidance, my instinct was to **tighten the reins**. Add more rules.
Draw firmer lines.
But it backfired.

Not because they were rebellious, but because they were *growing.*
They weren't toddlers needing timeouts, they were emerging adults learning to hear their own voices. And I had to learn a hard truth:
What worked when they were younger won't work now.
They don't need discipline, they need dialogue.
They don't need correction, they need connection.

That was tough for me, especially when their other parent seemed to let everything slide. We'd be holding the line, praying and parenting, and still hearing, "Y'all are doing too much." Meanwhile, we were left wondering, *Are we the only ones still expecting respect and responsibility?*

Here's what God had to work out in me:

Let Go of Ego. My style isn't the only "right" way, it's just the one I knew. But parenting isn't about proving a point. It's about building a relationship that lasts beyond rules.

Stop Parenting from Fear. Fear they'll fail. Fear they'll reject me. Fear they'll run too far. But fear leads to control. And control breaks connection. I had to learn to parent from *faith*, faith that what we've planted will bloom, even if it takes time.

Trust the Seeds We've Sown. *Proverbs 22:6* says, "Train up a child in the way he should go…" And we've done that. Maybe not perfectly, but prayerfully. Now I have to *trust the timing*, not just the training.

These days, I try to ask more questions than I give instructions.
I offer advice when invited, and grace even when it's not earned.
And when I pray, I don't ask God to make them obey, I ask Him to make *me* the kind of father they want to keep coming back to.

Because at the end of the day, **relationship outlasts rules**.
And presence will always speak louder than pressure.

She Says:

Can I be honest? I like structure. I'm that checklist-loving, rule-following, "where-are-you-going-and-what-time-will-you-be-back?" type of mom.

Stepping into this season of parenting young adults, where our kids suddenly need less direction and more space, has stretched me in every direction.

And it's even harder when the other parent (a.k.a. my ex) is... carefree. I'm talking, "If they mess up, they'll figure it out," or "You're too hard on them, just let them live."

At first, I was frustrated. Then I was defensive. Eventually, I was just exhausted.

But God reminded me, grace doesn't mean giving up standards. It means trusting God in the gray spaces.

Here's what I've been walking through:

Navigating a blended family can be challenging, especially when it comes to interactions with the other household. The temptation to compete for favor or to be the most lenient can be strong, but it's important to recognize that these efforts are not necessary. The key to successful co-parenting lies in being consistent, loving, and available. Consistency provides stability and predictability, helping children feel secure. Being loving means showing unconditional care and support, regardless of the circumstances. Availability ensures that we are present and attentive, ready to listen and engage when needed. By focusing on these principles, we create a nurturing environment that fosters healthy relationships and mutual respect, without the need for competition.

Parenting young adults is a delicate balance that calls for more prayer and less pressure. As they transition into adulthood, the role of a parent shifts from molding their character to mentoring their journey. The days of shaping their every decision are behind us; now, it's about guiding them with wisdom and love. Prayer becomes a vital tool, allowing us to seek divine guidance and strength as we support them. By releasing the need to control and instead focusing on mentoring, we create an environment where they can grow independently while knowing they have a steadfast support system. This approach fosters trust and respect, enabling them to navigate life's challenges with confidence and resilience.

Grace is often misunderstood as a sign of weakness, but in reality, it embodies profound strength. It takes immense courage to remain silent when our instinct is to intervene. It requires strength to listen attentively, offering a compassionate ear without judgment. Grace is the ability to say, "I trust you to figure it out, and I'm here if you need me," providing support without imposing solutions. This strength lies in recognizing that true growth comes from allowing others to face their challenges and learn from them. By extending grace, we empower those we love to develop their own resilience and wisdom, knowing they have a safe haven to return to when needed.
Don't compete with the other household. That was a tough one. But I had to realize, I don't have to be "the favorite" or the "most lenient." I just have to be consistent, loving, and available.

One verse that grounds me is James 1:5:
"If any of you lacks wisdom, let him ask God, who gives generously to all..."

I ask for wisdom daily. And when I don't know what to say, I speak blessings over them. When I don't know what to do, I trust that God is parenting them in ways I can't.

To all the blended families out there, and the parents trying to lead with love in a divided system: You are not failing because it's hard. You are faithful because you keep showing up.

We're learning to be more than disciplinarians, we're becoming safe spaces, wisdom holders, and grace givers. That's a parenting win, no matter how grown your kids are.

We Say:

Grace vs. Structure Conversation Guide

1. Set the Tone: Pray First
Begin by inviting God into the conversation. Ask for unity, wisdom, and clarity. A simple prayer might be:
"Lord, help us to listen with grace, speak with love, and lead with You at the center."

CONVERSATION STARTERS

Acknowledge Strengths

- "What do you think I do well as a parent?"
- "What are some strengths you bring that help keep our family steady?"

Goal: Celebrate each other's efforts. This builds trust and appreciation before addressing tension.

Identify the Tension

- "Where do you think we lean too heavily on structure?"
- "Where do you think we could offer more grace as the kids become adults?"

Goal: Invite honest reflection without blame. This is about awareness, not accusation.

Reflect on Your Upbringing

- "How did your parents handle rules, discipline, or mistakes?"
- "How do you think that shaped the way you parent today?"

Goal: Understanding the why behind your partner's parenting style can unlock deeper compassion.

Define Structure & Grace, Together

- "When you think of structure, what comes to mind?"

- "When you think of grace, how does that show up in parenting for you?"

Goal: Align on what these words mean to both of you, because definitions shape expectations.

MAKE IT PRACTICAL

Agree on a Parenting Philosophy Statement

Together, write a one-sentence "North Star" to guide your parenting. Example: "We will lead our children with love, using structure to protect and grace to empower."

Create a "Parenting Huddle" Rhythm

Set a regular time (biweekly or monthly) to check in about the kids, without the kids present.

Discuss:

- Wins and struggles
- Co-parenting challenges
- Where grace or structure might need to shift

Establish a "Grace Plan"

In moments where one parent feels the urge to discipline immediately, agree on a system:

- Pause before reacting
- Check in with each other first (if possible)
- **Ask:** "Is this a moment for correction, connection, or compassion?"

SPIRITUAL SUPPORT

Scriptures to Reflect on Together:

Ephesians 4:2 – "Be completely humble and gentle; be patient, bearing with one another in love."

Proverbs 22:6 – "Train up a child in the way he should go…"

Colossians 3:21 – "Fathers, do not embitter your children, or they will become discouraged."

James 1:5 – "If any of you lacks wisdom, let him ask God…"

Closing Reflections/Discussions:

- "In our current season, what does loving our children well look like, together?"
- "What do we need from each other to parent in unity, not just agreement?"

Chapter Nine:

"THROUGH IT ALL"

Question:

How can we keep our relationship strong during challenging times?

Our Story:

We've been through some things.

Real things.
Unexpected job losses.
Health scares. Hospitalizations.
Tense family dynamics.
Empty bank accounts.
Emotional exhaustion.
Ministry failures.
And seasons where it felt like the only thing holding us together was our wedding ring and the grace of God.

One particular season stands out.

We were both stretched thin. Emotionally drained. Financially tight. Spiritually weary. The kind of season where "I love you" sounds more like "Don't forget the bills" or "Did you follow up on that appointment?"

We weren't arguing, we were just disconnected. The weight of life was louder than the sound of us.

Then one night, in the middle of all the chaos, we turned off the TV, held hands, and just sat in silence. Then we cried. Prayed. And reminded each other: We're not enemies. We're not alone. We're still here. Together.

That night didn't change the circumstances, but it changed us. We realized strength isn't about avoiding storms, it's about holding on to each other when they come.

He Says:

I used to think that being strong meant carrying the weight of everything. If something went wrong, I'd go into "protection mode." Budget tighter. Work longer. Pray harder. Smile through the stress.

But what I've learned is this:
Strength in a relationship isn't just about surviving, it's about staying connected when everything around you feels unstable.

When the world is shaking, we have to be intentional about securing our foundation, not just our finances or feelings.

Here's what's helped us stay strong:

Stay spiritually synced. We pray together, even when it's awkward or short. Sometimes it's "Lord, help us not snap at each other today." That's real prayer too.

Keep showing up. Even if you don't know what to say or do-your presence matters more than your performance.

Laugh when you can. Sometimes we've laughed in the middle of a meltdown. It's therapy. It's holy. It reminds us that our bond is bigger than the moment.

Scripture says in Isaiah 43:2,
"When you pass through the waters, I will be with you…"
That reminds me: challenges don't cancel God's presence, and they don't cancel our covenant either.

Brothers, if life is heavy right now, don't run. Don't retreat. Lean in. Hold her hand. Pray like it matters. And remember: your relationship was built for more than just the easy days.

She Says:

Challenging times have a funny way of either pulling you apart or pressing you closer.

I've experienced both.

There were times I felt like saying, "Do you even see me in the middle of all this?" Not because he wasn't trying, but because life can be so loud that we stop noticing each other's quiet cries for connection.

Keeping a relationship strong during hard and challenging times requires a deep commitment to intentionality. When faced with adversity, it is easy to become overwhelmed and lose sight of the love that binds us. However, by being intentional in our actions and choices, we can navigate these difficult moments with grace and resilience. Intentionality means making a conscious effort to prioritize each other, even when external pressures threaten to pull us apart. It involves setting aside time for meaningful conversations, where we can express our fears, hopes, and dreams. By showing appreciation for each other, we reinforce the value of our relationship and remind ourselves of the reasons we chose to be together.

Supporting each other's dreams and aspirations is another crucial aspect of intentionality. During challenging times, it is important to stand by each other and offer encouragement and support. This not only strengthens our bond but also helps us grow individually and as a couple. Intentionality creates a safe space where love can flourish, even in the face of challenges. It reminds us that love is not just a feeling, but a series of deliberate acts that build a strong and lasting foundation. By being intentional, we can weather the storms of life together, emerging stronger and more united.

What's helped us stay strong?

Stay emotionally honest. I've learned to say things like, "I'm not mad, I'm just overwhelmed," or "I need 10 minutes of just being held." Those small confessions bring big healing.

Be each other's soft place. The world is hard enough. We try to make home feel like peace, not pressure.

Celebrate tiny wins. We thank God for making it through hard weeks, for unexpected provisions, and for moments of connection. Gratitude keeps us grounded.

One scripture I hold close is Galatians 6:2: "Carry each other's burdens, and in this way, you will fulfill the law of Christ."
That doesn't mean solving everything, it means saying, "You're not carrying this alone."

And to my sisters: even in hard seasons, you can still love deeply, pray fiercely, and speak gently. You can be strong together, even when everything around you feels uncertain.

Because when God is your anchor, storms don't destroy you, they develop you.

We Say:

Hard Season Survival Plan: A Relationship Toolkit for Tough Times

1. Pray First, Speak Second
"Lord, help us to see each other through Your eyes and hold each other with Your grace."

Before diving into deep or difficult conversations during challenging seasons, take a moment to pray together. It doesn't have to be long, just sincere. Inviting God into the moment can reset the tone and refocus your hearts.

2. Create a Shared "Peace Plan"
When everything feels chaotic, it helps to identify what brings calm. Ask each other:

- What helps you feel safe and grounded?
- What drains you when you're already stressed?
- What are 2 things I can do this week to help you breathe easier?

Write them down and revisit them weekly.

3. Choose Your Connection Ritual
Pick one small act of intentional connection you can commit to daily or weekly.

Options:

- A 30-second hug every morning
- A 10-minute check-in each evening ("What's one word to describe how you're feeling today?")
- A shared devotional or verse of the week

- A "no phones" walk or coffee time

Pro Tip: In crisis, little moments of connection matter more than grand gestures.

4. Schedule a Worry-Free Zone
Hard seasons can turn your relationship into a problem-solving boardroom. Give yourselves permission to pause the pressure.

Pick one time a week where you:

- Don't talk about bills, deadlines, or problems
- Watch a funny movie, play a game, or cook something new
- Remind each other what you like, not just what you lack

5. Speak Life, Even When It's Hard
During rough times, it's easy to criticize or shut down. Instead, try one of these phrases to keep your hearts open:

- "I'm with you, no matter what."
- "This is hard, but we are not breaking."
- "I don't have the words, but I'm here."
- "Thank you for staying present with me."
- "I love you, even on the hard days."

6. Scripture to Stand On (Together)

- **Romans 12:12** – "Be joyful in hope, patient in affliction, faithful in prayer."
- **Ecclesiastes 4:9-10** – "Two are better than one... if either of them falls, one can help the other up."
- **Isaiah 41:10** – "Do not fear, for I am with you..."
- **Philippians 4:13** – "I can do all things through Christ who strengthens me."

Try This: Write one verse on a sticky note and post it on the fridge, mirror, or phone screen each week as a reminder.

7. Ask for Help, Together

There's no shame in asking for support, spiritually or practically. Whether that's:

- Reaching out to a trusted mentor or counselor
- Asking a friend to pray for you both
- Delegating a responsibility that's too heavy right now
- You are not weak for needing help, you are wise.

8. Speak Hope Into the Future

Even when everything feels uncertain, speak faith into your tomorrow.

Finish this sentence together:

"No matter what happens, we're believing God will…"
(Examples: Provide / Strengthen us / Open a door / Restore peace / Heal our hearts)

Let that become your shared declaration.

Final Thought:

Hard times will come. But if you guard your unity, water your love, and keep God at the center, you won't just survive. You'll come out stronger, softer, and more deeply in love than before.

Chapter Ten:

"BEFORE YOU SAY 'I DO'"

Question:

What are signs of an unhealthy or abusive relationship?

Our Story:

It was supposed to be a joyful session.

We were meeting with a couple preparing for marriage. They were young, excited, deeply involved in their church, and already calling each other "my forever."

But the more we talked, the more something felt off.

She was quiet, overly careful with her words. He answered most of the questions, even the ones directed at her. When we discussed communication, conflict, and decision-making, his responses were confident, but controlling.

She laughed nervously at his dismissive comments. He jokingly called her "too emotional" and "too sensitive." But we weren't laughing.

The red flags weren't dramatic, they were subtle. But they were there:

He monitored her phone and social media.

He didn't want her spending time with her family unless he was present.

He made decisions for them, then asked her if she agreed.

She admitted to "walking on eggshells" when he was in a mood.

We asked them to pause the wedding planning and enter a season of serious counseling and accountability. It wasn't an easy conversation. But it was a necessary one.

Because love is not control. Love is not fear. Love is not manipulation.

Sometimes, the most loving thing you can do is **stop** a wedding before it becomes a marriage marked by harm.

Outside of this couple, in our own lives there were times when one of us talked over the other. Times when apologies were forced instead of freely given. Times when "I'm just being real" sounded a lot more like "I'm trying to dominate the conversation."

We weren't abusive, but we were dancing on the edge of something unhealthy. Thankfully, we had wise voices in our lives who helped us slow down, dig deeper, and deal with our emotional wounds before they became patterns.

Now, years later, after walking with couples in crisis and witnessing heartbreak up close, we're even more convinced of this truth:

Love doesn't control. It doesn't silence. It doesn't shame. Love doesn't hurt like that.

He Says:

As a man, a pastor, and a husband, I have to say this plainly:

Abuse is not love. Control is not leadership. Anger is not passion.

In that counseling session, I saw myself 15 years ago, before I knew how to handle emotions in a healthy way. Before I understood what it meant to be a servant leader and lover, not a dominating one. Back then, my responses were shaped by what I thought manhood was, loud, unbending, in control. But that wasn't strength, it was **toxic masculinity dressed as leadership**, and it lacked both godly wisdom and a healthy sense of identity. I had to unlearn the version of manhood I was taught or rather not taught and relearn what it means to lead with love, humility, and emotional maturity."

What I saw in that young man wasn't love, it was fear, insecurity, and the early signs of a destructive pattern.

Here's what I told him (and what I tell any man reading this):

If you feel the need to monitor her phone, that's not protection, it's possession.

If your tone makes her flinch, your words are already doing damage.

If your leadership makes her shrink instead of rise, it's not godly. It's toxic.

Ephesians 5 doesn't say to control your wife, it says to love her like Christ loved the church. That means sacrifice, humility, and creating safety.

To any couple reading this: Don't ignore the tension. Don't spiritualize dysfunction. Don't marry a version of someone you hope will change. God doesn't call us to endure abuse in the name of love. He calls us to truth, freedom, and peace.

Fellas, I want to be real with you.

There's a difference between leading and dominating. Between being passionate and being possessive. Between having high standards and having a controlling spirit.

If you're constantly raising your voice, tracking her phone, deciding who she can talk to, or making her feel like she has to "shrink" to keep peace, that's not godly manhood. That's a red flag.

I've counseled brothers who thought they were being "protective," but were actually being manipulative. I've seen men use Scripture to control, not cover. That's not biblical, it's spiritual abuse.

Ephesians 5:25 says, "Husbands, love your wives, just as Christ loved the church and gave himself up for her."

That means:
You lay down pride.
You listen without demanding agreement.
You create safety, not fear.

Let me say it plainly:
If you're in a relationship where love feels like walking on eggshells, that's not love, it's control in disguise.

She Says:

I knew something was wrong the moment she looked at him before answering almost every question. Not because she was unsure, but because she was afraid of saying the "wrong" thing.

As women, we're often taught to pray harder, love deeper, and submit more, even when the relationship is draining the life out of us.

But let me say this clearly, my dear sisters:
Submission is not silence. Love does not ignore warning signs. And God is not calling you to marry someone who mistreats you in private and smiles in public.

What broke my heart was how normal she thought this was.
She thought his control was love.
She thought his jealousy was protection.
She thought her anxiety was her problem, not a symptom of an unhealthy dynamic.

As women, we often excuse red flags in the name of loyalty, love, or potential.

We say things like:
"He's just passionate."
"He only gets like this when he's stressed."
"He's a good man deep down."

But sis, if you're constantly second-guessing your feelings, hiding bruises (physical or emotional), or shrinking who you are to keep the peace, it's not passion. It's not love. And it's not your job to "pray the abuse away."

1 Corinthians 13:5 says, "Love is not rude. It is not self-seeking. It is not easily angered. It keeps no record of wrongs."

Healthy love:
Let's you have a voice.
Doesn't punish you with silence or shame.
Doesn't make you afraid of "messing up."

Let me add:
Real love feels safe. Not perfect, but safe.
A healthy relationship makes room for your voice, your growth, and your God-given identity. And peace isn't something you manufacture, it's something you either experience… or you don't.

I told her what I wish more women would hear:

"You don't need a wedding date. You need wisdom." This statement underscores the importance of prioritizing wisdom over the rush to secure a wedding date. Wisdom involves understanding what constitutes a safe and healthy relationship, free from abuse. It means recognizing the signs of toxic behavior and knowing when to seek help. Wisdom empowers women to make informed decisions about their relationships, ensuring they are built on mutual respect, trust, and love. By focusing on wisdom, women can avoid the pitfalls of abusive relationships and create a foundation for a partnership that nurtures their well-being and growth. This approach emphasizes the value of emotional health and safety, reminding women that their **worth is not defined by a wedding date**, but by the strength and wisdom they bring to their relationships. If you're questioning the relationship, that's not weakness, that's wisdom knocking. Don't ignore it.

And please hear me:
God is not calling you to endure abuse in His name.
He's not asking you to cover up control with commitment.
And He will never bless what breaks you.

If you're seeing signs, get wise counsel. Get safe. And if necessary, get out.

You are God's daughter, and your safety is more important than saving face.

We Say:

🏴 Signs of an Unhealthy or Abusive Relationship (Checklist):
Use this list during engagement, or at any point, to evaluate what you're experiencing:

You feel anxious when your partner is upset.

Your voice, thoughts, or opinions are regularly dismissed.

There are rules about who you can talk to, where you can go, or what you can wear.

You're frequently blamed for their mood or anger.

You're isolated from friends or family.

You're made to feel "crazy," "too sensitive," or "disloyal" for bringing up concerns.

You experience physical intimidation, yelling, threats, or manipulation.

You feel like you're walking on eggshells more than walking in love.

If several of these sound familiar, it's time to pause. Seek help. Don't minimize it. Don't spiritualize it.

Scripture to Reflect On:
1 Corinthians 13:5 – "Love is not rude. It is not self-seeking. It is not easily angered."

2 Timothy 1:7 – "For God has not given us a spirit of fear…"

Proverbs 27:6 – "Wounds from a friend can be trusted…" (even hard truths during pre-marital counseling)

John 10:10 – "The thief comes only to steal and kill and destroy. I have come that they may have life…"

"Before You Say 'I Do'" Relationship Red Flag Inventory

Instructions:
Take this inventory privately or together. Be honest with yourself and with God. For each statement, answer: Yes (Y) No (N) Not Sure (N/S)

At the end, reflect on any patterns that point to unhealth, imbalance, or abuse.

Communication & Respect

- ☐ My voice and opinions are valued and heard.
- ☐ We can disagree without fear of backlash or belittling.
- ☐ I feel emotionally safe bringing up my concerns.
- ☐ My boundaries are respected without guilt or manipulation.
- ☐ I'm not pressured to say "yes" when I want to say "no."

Emotional & Spiritual Safety

- ☐ I feel loved, not controlled.
- ☐ My partner supports my personal and spiritual growth.
- ☐ I am not made to feel "crazy" or overly sensitive.
- ☐ We pray together in peace, not out of fear.
- ☐ I do not feel emotionally drained or constantly anxious in this relationship.

Control & Independence

- ☐ I have freedom in how I spend time, money, and communicate with others.
- ☐ My social media, phone, or privacy is respected.
- ☐ I am not isolated from family, friends, or my faith community.
- ☐ I do not feel like I'm being watched, tracked, or monitored.
- ☐ My partner does not make all the decisions without my input.

Conflict & Power Dynamics

- ☐ Disagreements don't lead to yelling, threats, or punishment.
- ☐ I'm not afraid of how my partner will react when things go wrong.
- ☐ I never feel physically intimidated or afraid to be myself.
- ☐ We take accountability for our actions rather than blaming each other constantly.
- ☐ My partner doesn't bring up my past to control me in the present.

Spiritual Maturity & Accountability

- ☐ My partner demonstrates the fruit of the Spirit (Galatians 5:22–23).
- ☐ We both submit to spiritual mentors, counseling, or pastoral leadership.
- ☐ We are open to correction and personal growth.
- ☐ Our faith walk strengthens our connection, not hides our dysfunction.
- ☐ There is mutual humility, not spiritual manipulation.

Reflection Questions:

- ☐ Were there multiple **N** or **N/S** responses in any one section?
- ☐ Did anything in this inventory make you feel uneasy or exposed something you've been ignoring?
- ☐ What support or counsel do you need to process these red flags further?
- ☐ Do you feel peace when you picture a future with this person, or tension?
- ☐ Are you staying in this relationship out of love, fear, pressure, or habit?

Final Encouragement:

God will never lead you into a relationship that causes you to lose your voice, question your value, or live in fear.

If red flags are present, pause. Seek wise counsel. Let your healing come before your vows. Love is patient, and that includes being patient enough to wait for what's healthy, whole, and heaven-sent.

You don't have to walk down the aisle to prove loyalty.
Your worth is not tied to a wedding date, it's anchored in Christ.

Chapter Eleven:

"STILL ME, STILL US"

Question:

How do we maintain individual identity in a relationship?

Our Story:

We didn't lose ourselves in love, but we almost misplaced ourselves in the marriage routine.

When we first got together, it was all about connection: date nights, deep talks, discovering what we both liked. But as time went on and life got louder, careers, changing parental roles, ministry, expectations, it became easy to trade individual identity for relational functionality.

One day, I (Dr. Ki) said, "I miss the old me. The nerdy bookworm me. The one who would go away alone just to be nothing to anybody."

And he said, "Funny... I was just thinking I haven't bowled in months or taken the long drive to sit alone by my prayer tree."

It wasn't that we were unhappy, it was that we were unintentionally blending into one version of "us" that didn't leave much room for me or you.

That moment launched a conversation, and a commitment:
We're better together when we stay whole as individuals.
Marriage didn't erase our uniqueness. It was meant to celebrate it.

He Says:

Look, I love my wife. I love our togetherness. But I also love the me God created.

And I had to learn, being "one" doesn't mean being identical.
We're one in purpose, one in heart, but still two people with different passions, callings, and quirks. And that's by design.

For a while, I felt guilty for wanting time to myself. To go for a solo drive. To bowl alone. To pursue a passion that wasn't part of "our" thing.

But I realized:
A healthy "we" needs a healthy "me."
If I abandon what makes me alive as a man, a friend, a son of God, I start running on empty. And an empty man makes a disconnected husband.

Here's what's helped me:

Stay connected to God first. Before I'm her husband, I'm His son. That keeps me rooted.

Keep my personal passions alive. Bowling. Fishing. Action movies with the sound bar on extra bass. They refuel me.

Encourage her individuality, too. Her thriving isn't a threat, it's a blessing to us both.

Jesus didn't call us to lose our identity in marriage. He called us to lay down selfishness, not personhood. Big difference

She Says:

I came into this marriage with both love and lessons.
After surviving a difficult divorce, I had seen firsthand what it looked like to lose yourself trying to hold something together. I knew what it felt like to carry the weight of unmet needs, misunderstood silence, and emotional exhaustion masked as faithfulness. When I said "yes" again, to love, to partnership, to covenant, I also made a quiet promise to myself: **I will not disappear in the name of being "good."**

I had to unlearn the belief that being a wife meant being *available at all times*, saying yes to everything, and molding myself to someone else's rhythm while abandoning my own.
This time, I was determined to show up differently.
Not guarded, but grounded.
Not fearful, but faithful.
Not perfect, but *present and whole.*

Over time, I realized that being a good wife isn't about performing. It's about being **authentic**, bringing the healed version of myself to the table, not just the helpful one. I don't have to overextend to prove my worth. I don't have to erase myself to be embraced. Love, real love, is not afraid of your fullness, it welcomes it.

God has been faithful in restoring my identity and even more faithful in teaching me how to protect it, not with walls, but with wisdom. In this marriage, I've learned that showing up as *me*, strong, spiritual, kind, and healed, is not only enough... it's necessary.
Because the woman I've become through the fire deserves to be seen, *even in love.*

It helped me that during my prayer time I heard the Holy Spirit whisper:

"I made you her before you became wife. You still get to be her."

I don't feel guilty when I bury myself in books for hours. When I call my "Best Fran – Dr. Thomosa – GG Dixon" just to laugh. When I go on a solo retreat to reconnect with God, not as "us," but as me.

And guess what? When I come back refreshed, rested, and full of joy… and our marriage was better.

Because here's the truth:
You can honor your marriage and still honor your individual soul.

Women, and even men, I suggest that you:
Define your identity beyond roles.
Set healthy boundaries. Time for yourself isn't selfish, it's soul care.
Cheer each other on. In our marriage - we don't compete, God completes, we complement, and that includes giving space to flourish individually.

One scripture that keeps me grounded is Psalm 139:14 –
"I praise you because I am fearfully and wonderfully made…"

That verse isn't revoked when you enter marriage. It's reinforced. God didn't create you to disappear, He created you to thrive.

Sis, hear this with love:
You don't have to lose you to love them. The best version of your marriage is one where you both bring your full, God-designed selves to the table.

We Say:

"Me, You, and Us" Reflection Journal Prompt

Me – Personal Identity Check-In (To be used by singles and couples)

Take a few minutes to reflect on who you are outside of your roles.

Answer honestly:

- What brings me joy just for me?
- What dreams or goals have I paused that I still feel drawn to?
- In what ways do I feel the most connected to God as an individual?
- When was the last time I did something that made me feel like myself?
- What parts of my identity have I allowed to fade, and why?

You – Celebrating Your Partner's Identity

Now shift your focus and reflect on what you admire and want to support in your partner:

- What unique gifts or passions do I see in my partner?
- Have I encouraged them to pursue the things that make them come alive?
- Do I listen when they express needs or desires that reflect their individuality?
- How can I support their spiritual and emotional growth this month?

Us – Growing Together While Staying Ourselves

Finally, bring it back to the relationship:

- How do we make space for both individuality and intimacy?
- Are we giving each other grace to grow outside of "us"?
- What rhythms or routines have caused us to unintentionally lose parts of ourselves?

- What's one thing we can each do this week to reconnect with our identity, and still strengthen our bond?
- What shared values hold us together even as we evolve?

Scripture to Reflect On:
"Two are better than one… If either of them falls down, one can help the other up." – **Ecclesiastes 4:9–10**
"I praise you because I am fearfully and wonderfully made." – **Psalm 139:14**

Final Thought:
A strong relationship doesn't require losing yourself, it invites you to bring your whole self to the table.

Celebrate who you are, honor who they are, and nurture the "us" that God is shaping through both.

Chapter Twelve:

"IT'S US FIRST"

Question:

What roles do family and friends play in a relationship?

Our Story:

From day one, we made a promise:
"This is our relationship. Our covenant. Our business."

Not in a secretive way, but in a sacred way.
We'd both been through seasons where family and friends meant well but meddled too much. We'd each felt the sting of broken trust, unsolicited opinions, and what happens when you let too many people have a front-row seat to your marriage.

When we first got together, we talked about it, seriously. We drew a line in love:

- ✓ We love our people.
- ✗ But they don't get to vote on how we do life together.
- ✓ We'll seek wise counsel.
- ✗ But we won't take emotional advice from someone whose life we wouldn't want to mirror.

And while we've had to lovingly remind a few folks of those boundaries over the years, the peace, protection, and unity it brought to our relationship has been worth every firm, prayer-covered "No, thank you."

He Says:

I love my family. I honor my friends. But I don't let either run my marriage.

One of the best decisions we ever made was setting clear expectations about what role other people would play in our relationship.

Here's what I've established as the non-negotiables:

Access is not entitlement. Just because someone is close to you doesn't mean they should be close to your conflicts or your covenant.

Advice should be invited, not assumed. I don't vent to everyone. If I need counsel, I select voices that are wise, married, and spiritually grounded.

My spouse comes before their opinions. Every time. If I have to choose between making them comfortable or protecting my wife's peace, you already know who wins.

Biblically, Genesis 2:24 says:
"A man shall leave his father and mother and be united to his wife, and the two shall become one flesh."

That's not just about leaving the house. It's about leaving emotional dependency. Leaving loyalty that gets in the way of intimacy. Leaving behind the need to please everyone but your partner.

No, every disagreement isn't a group chat moment. Not one frustration is a family debrief.

Some things are sacred. And sacred doesn't mean secret, it means protected.

She Says:

From the very beginning, I knew I wanted a relationship that was sacred, not public. Not secret, but *protected.*

I've always been a private person. Not because I'm hiding anything, but because I believe that real love grows best in quiet spaces, spaces where God is the loudest voice, and intimacy is nurtured without an audience.

I wasn't interested in building something that needed to be validated by outside opinions or constant commentary. I wanted a marriage where we could trust each other's hearts without third-party interpretation. A relationship grounded in **God, truth, and trust**, not in group chats or emotional spectators.

Not everyone needs to be invited into the inner workings of our covenant. Not because I don't value people, but because I value *us.*

And in a world where oversharing is the norm, I've learned that **preserving peace is a form of protection**.
Not every conversation needs a co-signer.
Not every disagreement needs a panel.

Sometimes the most powerful thing you can say is, *"Let's pray, not post."* This doesn't mean we walk alone. It means we walk **wisely**.

Because when your relationship is built on God's guidance, you don't need to be surrounded by noise, you just need to be covered in grace.

Here's what I teach to those I mentor:
Boundaries are not barriers, they're bridges to peace. They help define where others end and where our relationship begins.

Everyone doesn't get access to your intimate moments, good or bad. Some memories are just yours. Some arguments don't need a witness.

Honor your family, even your treasured friendships, but protect your marriage. You can love your mama and still not run back to her house every time things get hard.

One scripture that helps anchor boundaries with love is Proverbs 4:23: Above all else, guard your heart, for everything you do flows from it.

That includes guarding your marriage from too many voices, even well-meaning ones.

Let me also say this:
It's okay to re-train people as your relationship evolves. Some family and friends will need time to adjust. Some will test the boundaries. Be consistent. Be gracious. But don't bend.

You can say:
"We're still working through that privately, but thanks for caring."
"We've made a decision together that works for us."
"We love y'all, but we'll be handling this one as a couple."

Because at the end of the day, when the crowd quiets down, it's you and your person doing life together. So, build your home in peace. Invite love in, but protect your foundation with wisdom and prayer.

We Say:

"Boundaries in Love" Checklist

Conversation Starters

Take time together to reflect on and discuss each section. Use these to affirm your unity and adjust where needed.

Emotional Boundaries

- ✓ We've agreed that not every disagreement is shared with family or friends.
- ✓ We feel safe being vulnerable with each other without needing outside validation.
- ✓ We communicate frustrations directly to each other, not through third parties.
- ✓ We have a plan for who we seek wise, trusted counsel from, when needed.

Family Boundaries

- ✓ We've had an honest conversation about how much influence our families should have in our decisions.
- ✓ We both feel empowered to say, "Let's talk about that as a couple first."
- ✓ We've lovingly established limits around uninvited advice, drop-ins, or emotional pressure from family members.
- ✓ We agree to present a united front, especially when navigating differences with extended family.

Friendship Boundaries

- ✓ We do not allow friends to speak negatively about our partner or relationship.
- ✓ We balance our friend time with our couple time in a way that feels healthy.

- ✓ We've talked about what's appropriate to share with friends about our relationship.
- ✓ We both feel respected and supported in how we maintain our individual friendships.

Spiritual Boundaries

- ✓ We cover our relationship in prayer and invite God into our decisions first.
- ✓ We're both aware of when we need God's voice over group voices.
- ✓ We've discussed how to guard our relationship from religious pressure or spiritual manipulation (especially from others).
- ✓ We know when to seek biblical counsel versus emotional opinions.

Maintenance Plan: "Reset & Reaffirm"

- ✓ Schedule a relationship check-in every 3–6 months to:
- ✓ Reaffirm your boundaries
- ✓ Adjust what's no longer working
- ✓ Celebrate progress
- ✓ Pray together for continued protection and peace

Ecclesiastes 3:5 (paraphrased) – "There is a time to build... and a time to protect what's been built."

Reflection Prompt:

What's one boundary we've set that's really helped our relationship? Is there an area where we need to strengthen or reinforce a boundary right now?

Remember:

Healthy boundaries don't push people away, they keep your peace protected, your covenant strong, and your voices clear. You can honor others and honor each other.

Chapter Thirteen:

"WHEN WE DON'T SEE EYE TO EYE"

Question:

How can we handle disagreements about major life decisions?

Our Story:

We've always tried to pray before we plan, but that doesn't mean we always agree.

One of our biggest disagreements came when an opportunity arose, new job, new state, new everything. I saw purpose. He saw pressure. I called it a blessing. He called it a disruption. Neither of us was wrong, but we definitely weren't on the same page.

We tried to talk it out, but our "talks" quickly turned into tense silence and emotional shutdowns.

Then one night, after a particularly sharp exchange, we sat in the living room, quiet. No TV. No phones. Just two people who loved each other deeply but saw life very differently in that moment.

And we said four life-giving words:
"Let's pray, then talk."

That was the turning point. Not just because prayer changed our hearts (which it did), but because prayer reminded us, we were on the same team, even when we had different perspectives.

He Says:

Let me tell you, being the head of the household doesn't mean I get to overrule the house. Leadership in marriage isn't about making the final call. It's about making space for unity.

When we disagree about big things, finances, moves, career shifts, ministry roles, I've learned to:

Listen without defensiveness. Her "no" isn't disrespect, it's discernment.

Seek God's will over my own. Even if I want something badly, if there's no peace between us, it's not the right time.

Pause pride, invite wisdom. Proverbs 15:22 says, "Plans fail for lack of counsel, but with many advisers they succeed." Sometimes, we invite a trusted voice into the conversation, not to take sides, but to help us process.

When I choose patience over pressure, I'm honoring our covenant and God's timing.

Fellas, here's the real: If you want her trust, don't bulldoze your way through disagreement. Build understanding. Be willing to wait. And above all, pray like it matters. Because it does.

She Says:

Major life decisions can make you feel vulnerable. Will I be heard? Will my fears be honored? Will we really decide this together?

At times, I'd either shrink to keep the peace or push to get my point across. Neither worked.

What changed things for me was realizing:
We don't have to agree immediately, we just have to stay engaged lovingly.

Coming from a background where arguments turned into verbal attacks, or worse, disagreements used to feel dangerous to me.
I grew up around raised voices, broken promises, and people using love like a weapon. So when tension showed up in my adult relationships, I would either shut down to protect myself or overextend trying to fix it before it turned into something traumatic. But God, through His Word, therapy, and grace, began to heal those places in me.

I had to relearn – prior to this marriage - what conflict was *supposed* to look like in a healthy relationship. And what I discovered is that disagreement doesn't have to mean disrespect.
It doesn't have to end in disconnection.

In this marriage, we don't focus on needing to be "right" we focus on being **righteous in how we handle one another**. We are two different people with two different histories, perspectives, and communication rhythms. We're not always going to see things the same way right away.

But love doesn't demand instant agreement, it calls for *continual engagement.*
Not aggressive. Not passive. But **grace-filled**.

Now, instead of withdrawing or becoming emotionally overextended, I remind myself:

- We can pause without shutting down.
- We can disagree without dishonoring each other.
- We can stay in the room, not to prove a point, but to preserve the connection.

We don't need perfect alignment in every moment, we just need *mutual commitment* to keep showing up, keep listening, and keep loving, even through discomfort. Because in a relationship built on trust, we don't just fight for answers, we fight for *us.*
And that kind of love?
It's not just healing.
It's holy.

A few things that helped us:
Speak with clarity, not combat. Saying, "I feel unsure because…" is better than "This is a terrible idea!"

Find the shared value beneath the disagreement. Sometimes we both want the same thing (security, peace, purpose) but see different paths to get there.

Stay prayerful and practical. I ask God, "Help me hear **Your voice, and his**."

Sister Gals, speak up. Listen well. Trust God more than your comfort. And know this, disagreement isn't defeat. It's just part of the journey to deeper unity.

We Say:

"Disagree in Peace" Discussion Tool

Step 1: Pray First
Start by inviting God into the process, together.
Even a simple prayer like:

"Lord, help us listen with love, speak with grace, and choose unity over ego."

Step 2: Identify the Issue Clearly

? "What exactly are we trying to decide?"

? "Why is this decision important to each of us?"

Write the issue down in one sentence. Be specific and stay focused.

Step 3: Take Turns Sharing (Without Interrupting)
Each partner gets 3–5 uninterrupted minutes to respond to the following prompts:

- "Here's what I believe is the best decision…"
- "Here's why this matters to me personally or spiritually…"
- "Here's what I fear, hope for, or need in this situation…"

Switch roles after the first person finishes.
Take a deep breath, **no rebuttals yet. Just receive.**

Step 4: Reflect Back What You Heard
Each of you now takes a turn saying:

- "What I hear you saying is…"
- "I didn't realize you felt ___; thank you for sharing that."

This helps you move from defense to understanding.

Step 5: Find the Shared Values
Look for the "why" beneath the surface disagreement. Use prompts like:

- "Even though we see it differently, it sounds like we both care about…"
- "Our shared goal in this is…"

Write your shared values down. These are your anchor points during uncertainty.

Step 6: Agree on the Next Right Step

- "What can we do today that honors both of our perspectives?"
- "Do we need to pause? Pray longer? Seek counsel? Clarify logistics?"

Choose unity over urgency. A good decision will wait for mutual peace.

Scripture to Stand On Together:

- **James 1:5** – "If any of you lacks wisdom, let him ask of God…"
- **Proverbs 3:5-6** – "Trust in the Lord with all your heart…"
- **Philippians 2:2** – "Be like-minded, having the same love…"

Closing Check-In:
Finish the conversation with this shared statement:

"We're still on the same team, even when we don't agree. We're choosing peace, prayer, and partnership as we walk this out."

Chapter Fourteen:

"THE PAST, THE PAIN, AND THE PEACE"

Question:

What are the impacts of past relationships on our current one?

Our Story:

We didn't walk into this marriage empty-handed, we walked in with history.

Not just emotional baggage, but also wisdom, wounds, lessons, and a whole new level of self-awareness. We had both been married before. We had both been hurt before. And we had both promised ourselves that if we ever got married again, it would be different.

And it has been… but not without doing some hard soul work.

We came into our relationship with:

Fears of repeating past mistakes

Guarded trust

Guilt from how things ended

And still, an occasional need to interact with our ex-spouses, respectfully, for the sake of peace and family

There were moments when the old pain whispered lies. Times when triggers made us question if healing had really happened. But through grace, truth, and a whole lot of prayer, we learned how to move forward without punishing each other for the past.

He Says:

The truth? My past relationship left a mark.

Not because I haven't forgiven. Not because I'm still holding on. But because everything I went through shaped how I show up now.

After my divorce, I promised myself I would never:
Shut down emotionally
Make peace the priority over communication
Let resentment simmer until it turned into silence

But when we got married, I still caught myself doing those things. Not because she deserved it, but because I hadn't learned to fully trust love again.

I thank God every day that this marriage is a space where we can talk about the past without shame. Where triggers aren't treated like weaknesses. And where healing isn't rushed, it's respected.

Here's what's helped me:

Own my healing. It wasn't her job to fix what someone else broke.

Talk about triggers, not just react to them.

Keep the past in perspective. I don't bring it into every disagreement, but I don't pretend it didn't happen either.

Spiritually, I lean on Isaiah 43:18–19: Forget the former things; do not dwell on the past. See, I am doing a new thing! God didn't just give me a new marriage, He gave me a new mindset.

And when I interact with my ex now, it's from a place of respect, not resentment. Because I've been healed enough to leave bitterness behind and walk in peace.

She Says:

He Didn't Deserve to Pay for Their Sins, So I Did the Work to Be Whole There was a time, long before we ever met, when I honestly believed,
"I'll never trust anyone again."

After surviving childhood trauma and navigating a painful, draining divorce, I wasn't just wounded, I was weary. Love sounded beautiful in theory, but risky in practice. And for a long while, I couldn't tell if I was protecting my heart… or just hiding it behind fear.

But somewhere along the journey, I made a decision: If I ever loved again, it would be from a healed place, not a hurting one. I owed that to myself. And I owed that to the man I hadn't even met yet, because he shouldn't have to bleed for wounds he didn't cause.

When we finally met, something in me was ready. Not perfect. Not polished. But *prepared.* He wasn't a savior, I already had One.
He was a partner. A safe space. A steady presence.

And because I had done the work beforehand, through **prayer, therapy, accountability, and intentional healing**, I was able to recognize that what we had was healthy… even if my past still tried to whisper otherwise.

Were there moments when my trauma tried to resurface? Yes.

- Times I braced for abandonment that wasn't coming.
- Times I mistook silence for punishment.
- Times I overreacted, not because of what he did, but because of what I had once endured.

But here's what changed the game:
He didn't shame me for needing reassurance.
He didn't punish me for my past.
And because I had already *faced* that past, it didn't get to rule our present.

Here's what helped me stand in freedom:
Therapy and prayer. Jesus saved my soul. Counseling helped untangle my story. I needed *both.*
Speaking truth to fear. I had to say out loud, "This is not that. He is not them. I am not who I used to be."
Healthy boundaries with my past. We co-parent and communicate where necessary, but I don't reopen doors that God has closed.

The Scripture that carried me through was **Joel 2:25**: *"I will restore to you the years the locust has eaten…"*
And He did.

God didn't just restore my hope, He gave me a relationship where love could grow in **safe soil**.

Where honesty is honored, grace is mutual, and healing is a shared language, not a hidden secret.

To my sisters who have walked through pain and are hoping for love again:

You don't have to rush. But you do have to heal.
Do the work. Tell the truth. Let God in.
Because when you do, love won't have to break you to build you, it will meet you where you're whole.

We Say:

"Then vs. Now" Healing Inventory

Start With Prayer
"God, thank You for bringing us into a new season. Help us reflect honestly on what we've experienced, grow from what we've learned, and love each other with maturity and grace."

Step 1: Personal Reflection – "Then"
Take a moment individually (or together) to reflect on your previous relationship(s). Be honest without reliving the pain.

Answer the following:

- ? What patterns from my past relationship affected me the most?
- ? What wounds still need healing?
- ? What triggers or fears still show up for me occasionally?
- ? How did my previous relationship shape my view of love, trust, or conflict?

Step 2: Present Awareness – "Now"
Now reflect on how you're growing and showing up differently in your current relationship:

- ? What are 3 ways I've grown since my last relationship?
- ? How has this current relationship helped me heal?
- ? What new strengths or habits am I learning as a partner?
- ? What are we doing differently, and more intentionally, this time?

Step 3: Discussion Questions (For Both Partners)
Use these to foster understanding and connection:

? What's one fear or wound I brought into our relationship that you've helped me with?
? What's something I'm still working on that I'd like you to be patient with?

? What's a healthy boundary we've set that protects our peace, especially when it comes to ex-spouses or old memories?
? How can we support each other in continuing to grow, heal, and move forward together?

Step 4: Restoration Declaration
Say this out loud together or personalize it in your own words:

"This is not that. We are not who we were. We are choosing to build something new, anchored in love, covered by grace, and strengthened by God. The past has shaped us, but it does not define us. We are growing, healing, and walking forward, together."

Scriptures to Reflect On:

- **Isaiah 43:18–19** – "Forget the former things… See, I am doing a new thing!"
- **Joel 2:25** – "I will restore to you the years that the locust has eaten…"
- **2 Corinthians 5:17** – "If anyone is in Christ, he is a new creation…"

Healing is a journey, and your willingness to grow together, not just move on, is what makes this love different.

Chapter Fifteen:

"SAME FAITH, DIFFERENT FILTERS"

Question:

How can we navigate differences in beliefs and values, even when we share the same spiritual foundation?

Our Story:

We love God. We believe the Bible. We're committed to following Christ, together.

And still… we don't always see things the same way.

We've always been aligned on the big things:
We believe in God.
We believe in giving.
We believe that everything we have belongs to Him.

When it came to tithing, sowing, and living generously, even during tight seasons, we were already on the same page.
But **shared faith doesn't always mean identical decisions**, especially when it comes to *how* that faith is expressed.

The tension started when she came to me with an idea she believed God had placed on her heart:
"Let's shut down regular church every fourth Sunday and take the ministry into the community."
Worship through outreach.
No offering plates.
No formal service.
Just food, prayer, connection, and meeting real needs outside the four walls.

It sounded noble. It was definitely needed. But it also sounded *financially risky*, especially at a time when the church was already feeling the strain. We were trying to keep the lights on, pay rent, and stretch every dollar. Every Sunday counted. Every offering mattered.

And while neither of us questioned the heart behind the idea, we both knew what it could cost.

She was confident. She had clarity.
"This is what God said," she told me.

So, while I was supportive, I'll be honest, I was nervous.
Not because I didn't believe in outreach, but because I couldn't yet see the provision that would meet us on the other side of that obedience.
But we did it anyway.
One month at a time.
One outreach at a time.

And the outcome?
It didn't make sense *on paper*, but it made an impact on *people*.
We fed families during food insecurity.
We prayed with people who wouldn't walk through church doors.
We gave clothes, gas, school supplies, and comfort when life was giving people very little to hold onto.

Every time we stepped into the streets, **God stepped in behind us.**
And slowly, we watched something beautiful happen:
Ministry multiplied.
Resources stretched.
People gave, not just money, but time, love, and hands.

We didn't just grow as a church. We grew as a couple.
We learned that obedience doesn't always come with agreement first, but when it's *God-ordained*, it will produce fruit.

Yes, we were both nervous.
But she had heard clearly, and I had to trust her hearing.
That season taught us that faith isn't always comfortable. But when you're committed to each other and submitted to God, **obedience opens doors that fear would have kept shut.**

He Says:

Her Obedience Challenged My Comfort, But It Also Strengthened My Faith Let me tell you, just because you believe in the same God doesn't mean you always agree on how to walk that faith out. And honestly? That's okay.

Marriage isn't about mirroring each other's every move. It's about covenant. We both bring different histories, convictions, and callings into how we live out what we *both* believe. And one of the biggest lessons I had to learn in this area was this: **Just because I'm uncomfortable doesn't mean she didn't hear from God.**

When my wife came to me and said, *"We're supposed to shut down church on the fourth Sunday every month and take ministry into the community,"* I had questions. Real ones. Not because I didn't believe in outreach. But because we were already walking a tight financial line.

As a pastor, I felt the weight of stewardship. As a husband, I felt the pressure of provision. As a man, I felt stretched between faith and fear. But what I saw in her was **certainty, not stubbornness**. She wasn't reacting emotionally, she was responding in obedience. And even though I was uneasy, I knew I couldn't dismiss what God had deposited in her spirit.

Ultimately, I made a choice.
To lean in, not pull back.
To partner with her, even in my hesitation.
To trust that if God was speaking to *her*, He'd stretch *me* in the process.

Here's how I've learned to navigate our differences:

Respect the way she hears from God. Her approach may be different than mine, but her discernment is sharp. When she says, "God said," I've learned to pause and pay attention. Listen to the "why" behind her values. Usually, what she values most reveals something deep about her story or relationship with God.

Surrender pride to protect peace. It wasn't easy admitting I was nervous. But unity doesn't come from pretending. It comes from honesty, and letting love lead through the uncertainty. In checking my pride. I had to learn to say, "I see it differently, but I still respect you."

Pray for alignment, not control. Romans 12:10 says, *"Honor one another above yourselves."* That means honoring her vision, even when I can't see it all yet. God honors that kind of humility. That includes her perspective, even when I don't fully agree.

In the end, those outreach Sundays didn't break us, they *built* us.
They grew our faith.
They deepened our trust.
And they reminded me that leadership doesn't always look like being in the front. Sometimes, it looks like saying, "I trust God in you."

Ultimately, I don't want to win debates, I want us to grow together.

God didn't call us to conformity. He called us to unity. And I'd rather stretch together than settle apart.

She Says:

Obedience Wasn't Up for Debate, But Unity Was Still My Goal. When we got married, I already knew that agreeing on faith didn't mean we'd agree on *everything*. Same God, same beliefs, same direction. Completely different people.

From day one, I made it clear, **honoring the voice of God would always be my first priority.** Not out of rebellion. Not out of pride. But because I've learned, through pain, through wilderness seasons, through watching promises unfold, that obedience to God isn't just sacred… it's survival.

When God spoke to my heart and told me to shut down regular church service on the fourth Sunday each month and turn that time into community outreach, I didn't flinch spiritually, but I did pause relationally. Because I knew what I heard… but I also knew what it *could cost*. Financially. Logistically. Emotionally.

And I also knew I needed to present it to my husband with *both boldness and humility*. Not to get his permission to obey God, but to invite him into the journey *with me*, not after me.

We were already in a tight financial season.
It didn't look like the "right time."
But obedience rarely does.

And though he was hesitant, and honestly, so was I, we chose to trust that **if God gave the instruction, He would supply the outcome.** We prayed. We talked. We stretched.

And the fruit? The outreach not only touched the community, it transformed *us*. Because even though we had the same faith, our values got tested in how we *lived it out.*

Here's some wisdom:

Obedience to God doesn't cancel respect for your spouse. I didn't bulldoze my way forward. I brought the vision, the conviction, and the clarity to him in love. And I trusted that God would bring us into unity, even if it came step by step.

Ask for clarity, not control. I stopped interpreting hesitation as opposition. Instead, I asked him questions like, "What are your concerns?" and "What do you need to feel peace about this?"

Look for your shared "why." Even when our approaches looked different, our *heart* was the same, we both wanted to honor God and serve people well. That made it easier to find agreement beyond method.

Protect peace, not preference. Colossians 3:14 says, *"Above all, put on love, which binds us together in perfect unity."* That unity isn't built on identical views, but on mutual grace.

The truth is, differences in belief application aren't always a threat. Sometimes, they're a **divine invitation**, to trust deeper, to listen harder, and to love past our own perspectives.

To the wives (and husbands) navigating faith-driven tension:
Be kind. Be bold. Be submitted to God *and* respectful in partnership.
You're not just building a house of agreement.
You're building a house of faith, wisdom, and understanding.
And that's the kind of house God can *dwell in.*

And one more thing, if you find yourself always at war with someone you're supposed to be walking with, constantly

clashing instead of growing, ask yourself, "Is this a God-ordained connection, or a forced one?"

Healthy love won't always be easy, but it shouldn't always feel like battle. When it's God, there will be peace *even in the stretch.*

We Say:

Core Values Clarity Exercise

Step 1: Pray for Clarity & Humility
"Lord, help us understand each other beyond words. Give us grace to honor what we both value, and wisdom to build unity even where we differ."

Step 2: Define Your Personal Values
Individually, take a few moments to write down your top 5–7 personal values.n(Examples: Integrity, Honesty, Generosity, Stability, Flexibility, Faith, Family Time, Simplicity, Discipline, Hospitality)

My Top Personal Values Values	My Partner's Top Personal
1.	1.
2.	2.
3.	3.
4.	4.
5.	5.
6. (optional)	6. (optional)
7. (optional)	7. (optional)

Step 3: Compare & Discuss
Ask each other:

- ? Where do we align?
- ? Where do we differ?
- ? Which value surprised you the most from my list?
- ? How do you see me living out my values? Where could I grow?
- ? Have our differences in values caused tension before? How did we handle it?

Step 4: Apply It to Real-Life Situations

Choose 1–2 past or current decisions where tension showed up (parenting, giving, spending, serving, etc.). For each one:

- ? What value was most important to you in that moment?
- ? What value do you think was most important to your spouse?
- ? How could you have honored both values in a unified way?

Example:
Topic: Giving to a friend in need
Your value: Stewardship
Spouse's value: Generosity
Shared solution: Prayerfully give a partial amount together and revisit the rest in a week.

Step 5: Create a Shared Values Statement

Write a one-sentence summary of how you will honor your differences and walk in unity.

Example: "We will honor each other's convictions, ask for understanding before assuming, and seek God's wisdom as we make decisions that reflect both our hearts."

Scriptures to Meditate On:

- **Romans 14:19** – "Let us make every effort to do what leads to peace and mutual edification."
- **Colossians 3:14** – "And over all these virtues put on love, which binds them all together in perfect unity."
- **Proverbs 4:7** – "Wisdom is the principal thing; therefore get wisdom: and with all thy getting get understanding."

This exercise helps make the invisible visible, turning silent values into spoken understanding, and building a relationship where faith and love lead the way.

Chapter Sixteen:

"YOUR WIN IS MY WIN"

Question:

What are the best ways to support each other's growth and goals?

Our Story:

From day one, we made a vow beyond the altar:
We will never compete; God completes, we will always find ways to complement.

That was important because our journeys weren't identical. I (Dr. Ki) had already earned multiple college degrees, including a doctorate. I had years of academic and professional experience under my belt. He didn't have a degree, and honestly, I didn't need him to have one to validate his value. I married the man, not the résumé.

But I always saw more in him.

Not in a "fixer" kind of way, but in a faith-in-you kind of way. He was gifted, wise, and full of untapped potential. I never pushed, but I did pray. And one day, he said,
"I think I'm ready."

What followed was a journey we walked together: him back in school, me cheering from the sidelines (and proofreading the occasional paper), him juggling classes and work, me holding space for his growth with joy, not jealousy.

When he walked across that graduation stage, I clapped like I was the one receiving the degree. Because in a covenant like ours, his victory was my victory too.

He Says:

Let me say this plainly: She never made me feel less than.

Not once.

I knew she had more education. More professional credentials. But she never used that to diminish me, she used it to lift me.

And that kind of support? It changed everything.

She didn't nag. She didn't guilt me. She simply made space for me to grow, and spoke life into places I had almost abandoned.

Here's what helped me thrive:

She encouraged without pressure. Her belief in me was quiet, consistent, and powerful.

We celebrated each other's lanes. I didn't need to be her academic match, I just needed to be present, growing, and walking in purpose.

She gave me room to evolve. I was never treated like a "project", I was treated like a partner with promise.

Spiritually, I held tight to Philippians 1:6:
"He who began a good work in you will carry it on to completion…"

And He did. Through my wife's support, God reminded me that my story wasn't done. And that no matter where I started, my future was still full of purpose

She Says:

We decided that growth wouldn't be a competition, it would be a covenant. In our marriage, we made a decision early on: we would grow together, not compete with each other. We didn't have the same backgrounds, the same educational paths, or the same strengths, but we did have the same heart posture: to see each other win. I didn't need him to be "impressive" on paper, I needed him to be intentional in purpose.

That's how we kept our relationship healthy, even when our accomplishments came at different paces, in different seasons, and through different doors.

Yes, I had degrees. But love isn't about degrees, it's about destiny alignment. And I knew his life carried weight, calling, and depth, regardless of diplomas.

I never pushed him toward school. But I did speak to the greatness I saw in him. And when he said he was ready to pursue more? I moved into position as his biggest cheerleader.

What helped us grow together:

We honored each other's lanes. I never expected him to walk my journey, or to mirror my path just to make things look balanced on paper. He had his own road, his own rhythm, and his own revelation of what success looked like. So instead of trying to pull him into my lane, I learned how to walk *alongside* him. To cheer him on when the world didn't see him. To pray for him when he doubted himself. And to remind him that who he was becoming mattered more than how fast he got there. And he did the same for me.

We prioritized partnership over ego. I've been blessed to pursue higher education, multiple degrees, and professional milestones. But I never used those accomplishments as leverage in our home. **I celebrated what I achieved without shrinking who I loved.** He never made me feel like I needed to downplay my voice or dim my light to preserve his confidence. Instead, he protected it. Covered it. Amplified it. Because he knew my wins didn't threaten him, they *represented us.* And I honored him just the same. Whether he was in a season of building, rebuilding, or standing still, I never measured his worth by his résumé. I measured it by his heart, his integrity, and his commitment to keep growing. I celebrated him without shrinking myself. He did the same.

We made growth a shared mission. If it mattered to one of us, it mattered to *both* of us. If one of us was called to stretch, the other showed up with support, not sarcasm. When he returned to school to pursue his degree later in life, we adjusted our rhythm. We prayed, sacrificed, and celebrated *together.* Because when you're in covenant, **your partner's progress is your praise report too.**

One verse that guides us is Ecclesiastes 4:9–10: "Two are better than one… If either of them falls down, one can help the other up."

Marriage isn't about outpacing each other, it's about outlasting challenges together.

So, to every wife cheering on her husband: your encouragement is not small. Your belief is not background noise. It's life-giving.

And to every couple walking at different paces, just remember: if you're walking in the same direction, you're winning.

To anyone wondering how to support each other's growth without losing yourself in the process:
Celebrate them *without comparison.*
Cheer for each other *without competition.*

And remember, **real love is never intimidated by progress. It's inspired by it.**

We Say:

Growth Goals as a Team: Planning Sheet

Step 1: Begin with Prayer
"Lord, help us to see the greatness You've placed in each other. Teach us to support with joy, not comparison. Remind us that we are one in purpose, even when our goals are different."

Step 2: Identify Individual Growth Goals
Take turns answering the following:

Partner 1 – My Growth Goals
One personal or spiritual goal I want to pursue this year is:
➤ ____

Why it matters to me:
➤ ____

How I'd love to be supported as I pursue this:
➤ ____

Partner 2 – My Growth Goals
One personal or spiritual goal I want to pursue this year is:
➤ ____

Why it matters to me:
➤ ____

How I'd love to be supported as I pursue this:
➤ ____

Step 3: Identify Shared Growth Goals
What are some things we want to grow in together?

Spiritually (example: daily prayer, Bible reading, fasting together)
➤ ____

Financially (example: saving for a home, paying off debt, giving goals)
➤ ____

Relationally (example: better communication, more date nights, a marriage retreat)
➤ ____

As a family or ministry team (example: serving together, raising children in faith)
➤ ____

Step 4: Check-In Conversation Starters
Use these prompts monthly or quarterly to stay connected and supportive:

- "What's one thing you're excited about in your growth right now?"
- "Is there any way I can support you more or differently?"
- "What's something we can celebrate from this past month?"
- "Where can we realign if we've gotten off track?"

Encouragement Declaration
Say or write this together:

"We are not in competition, we are in covenant. We celebrate, support, and stand by each other as we grow. Your win is my win, and our journey is sacred. We will keep moving forward, side by side."

Scriptures to Stand On

- **Ecclesiastes 4:9** – "Two are better than one, because they have a good return for their labor."
- **Philippians 1:6** – "He who began a good work in you will carry it on to completion…"
- **Romans 12:10** – "Be devoted to one another in love. Honor one another above yourselves.

Chapter Seventeen:

"BUSY, BUT STILL US"

Question:

How can we make time for each other with a busy schedule?

Our Story:

We used to say, "This week looks crazy, but next week will be calmer."

And then… next week got crazier.

Between full-time careers, ministry obligations, mentoring others, showing up for our adult children, and still trying to sleep more than five hours, we realized something: margin wouldn't happen by accident. We had to make room for each other on purpose.

There was a stretch where we were ships passing in the night. Serving others all day, pouring out everywhere else, and quietly missing each other in the process.

One day, we sat at dinner and realized we hadn't laughed, really laughed, in weeks. Not because we weren't okay… but because we weren't connecting.

We did something radical:
We scheduled each other. And we didn't feel bad about it.
Not because it was forced, but because it was faithful and fruitful.

He Says:

Let me be real, life gets loud.

When you're leading, serving, parenting, and providing, it's easy to look up and realize you've been loving the whole world... except your spouse.

That realization hit me like a ton of bricks. I wasn't trying to neglect her, I was just stretched thin. But God reminded me:

Your marriage isn't just a priority, it's part of your purpose.

I stopped treating quality time like a luxury. I started treating it like a lifeline.

Here's what's worked for us:

Scheduled check-ins. We protect time, even if it's 30 minutes. If it's on the calendar, it happens.

Mini-moments matter. Prayer in the car. Laughing while folding clothes. Holding hands at the grocery store. Those things count.

Sabbath mindset. We intentionally carve out one day a week with no ministry or work meetings. That's sacred.

One verse that anchors me is Mark 6:31 –
"Come with me by yourselves to a quiet place and get some rest."

If Jesus Himself called His disciples to pause and recharge, surely we need to protect moments to reconnect.

Because no ministry, no meeting, no deadline is more important than this covenant right here.

She Says:

I love what we do. I love who we serve. But I love us more, and I don't want to be in a marriage where we minister together publicly but feel disconnected privately.

There was a season where I'd look at him across the pulpit… but miss him across the dinner table.

That's when I realized, we can't just exist beside each other. We have to keep pursuing each other.

Here's what's helped me:

Give grace for capacity. Some weeks we have time for a full date night. Some weeks, it's takeout and 15 minutes of eye contact. Both are wins.

Creative connection. We've had date night at home with pajamas and popcorn. We've done walk-and-talks. We've left voice memos during the day. We make it work. Quickies can be just as memorable as all-night sessions.

In the past, I would hold it in, waiting for him to notice I was off. I'd walk around frustrated, feeling disconnected, all while silently hoping he'd read my mood and respond accordingly. But I've learned that **stewing in silence builds resentment, not connection.** Now, I practice speaking the need with clarity and kindness. Not in accusation. Not with attitude. But with vulnerability.

I simply say:
"I miss you. Can we carve out some time for just us?"

Those words don't just request time, they *invite closeness.*
They say: *You matter. We matter. I still want you.*

And more often than not, that gentle honesty opens the door to intimacy, emotionally and even physically. Because here's the truth: **Intimacy doesn't begin in the bedroom, it begins in conversation.** It begins in the courage to express, "I need you," without shame. In the humility to admit, "I feel distant," without blame. And in the faith that if you say what's real, love will meet you there.

Now, instead of withdrawing, I reach. Instead of assuming, I ask. And instead of waiting for connection to magically happen, I plant the seed with simple words, and let God or strategically placed kisses water the rest.

One scripture I hold onto is Song of Solomon 2:15 – "Catch the little foxes that spoil the vine…" Because sometimes, it's the small distractions that quietly steal closeness.

To every couple juggling everything, your schedule may be full, but don't forget to make room for each other. Even in chaos, connection is possible.

We Say:

Connection Calendar: Making Room for "Us" on Purpose

Start With Prayer
"Lord, help us to see each other through Your eyes. Teach us to protect our time together and show us how to love each other well in every season."

Step 1: Define What Connection Looks Like in This Season
Use this space to talk about what "connection" means for each of you right now, emotionally, spiritually, and physically.

I feel most connected when we:

➤ ______________________________

Right now, I need more:

➤ [ ] Quality conversation
➤ [ ] Physical closeness
➤ [ ] Spiritual unity
➤ [ ] Rest/relaxation time
➤ [ ] Laughter or fun
➤ [ ] Something else: _________

Step 2: Review Your Week Together
Pull out a calendar and walk through the upcoming week. Mark:

- Non-negotiables (work, church, parenting responsibilities)
- Flexible blocks
- Shared time opportunities

Step 3: Schedule "Connection Moments"

Day	Connection Moment	Time/Details
Monday	[ ] Walk and pray together	7:00–7:30 PM
Tuesday	[ ] Text a verse + encouragement	During lunch
Wednesday	[ ] Shared devotional	Morning before work
Thursday	[ ] Quick check-in: "How's your heart?"	9:00 PM
Friday	[ ] Couch movie date	8:30 PM
Saturday	[ ] Lunch or coffee out	12:00 PM
Sunday	[ ] Pray before service	9:00 AM

Note: Don't aim for perfection. Aim for presence. Even short moments matter when they're intentional.

Step 4: Build Your "Love in the Margins" List

Use this when life feels too full for planning, quick ideas for spontaneous connection:

- ✓ Voice memo of encouragement
- ✓ "I'm thinking about you" text
- ✓ Five-minute forehead-to-forehead prayer
- ✓ One-song slow dance in the living room
- ✓ Leave a sticky note on their mirror
- ✓ Pick up their favorite snack "just because"

Connection Declaration

Say this together at the start of the week:

"We choose each other. In the middle of busy, we make space for love. God is our center, and we are one, through every full calendar, we remain close, connected, and committed."

Scripture to Anchor Your Week

- **Mark 6:31** – "Come with me by yourselves to a quiet place and get some rest."

- **Ecclesiastes 4:9–10** – "Two are better than one… if either falls, one can help the other up."
- **1 Peter 4:8** – "Above all, love each other deeply…"

^b

Preparing for Connection Inventory – For Singles

"Am I emotionally, spiritually, and relationally ready to connect in a healthy, God-honoring way?"

🕮 *Foundational Scripture:*

Proverbs 4:23 (NLT) – *"Guard your heart above all else, for it determines the course of your life."*

SECTION 1: Heart & Healing Check

Rate each statement from 1–5

(1 = Not true at all, 5 = Completely true)

Statement	**Rating**
I've taken time to heal from past heartbreaks or toxic relationships.	☐
I've forgiven myself and others for past emotional pain.	☐
I've identified unhealthy patterns in how I've connected with others.	☐
I'm not looking for a relationship to fix or validate me.	☐
I'm able to communicate my needs clearly and respectfully.	☐

Reflection: What are 1–2 areas where you may need more healing or clarity?

SECTION 2: Spiritual Alignment & Discernment

Statement	**Rating**
I actively seek God's direction before pursuing or entertaining relationships.	☐
I'm willing to walk away from connections that disrupt my peace or pull me away from purpose.	☐

Statement	Rating
I have a consistent prayer life and quiet time with God.	☐
I know the difference between godly standards and superficial preferences.	☐
I understand what spiritual alignment in a partner means, and why it matters.	☐

Reflection: How are you spiritually preparing for a relationship?

SECTION 3: Emotional Maturity & Availability

Statement	Rating
I am self-aware and can manage my emotions in a healthy way.	☐
I do not let fear of abandonment or rejection dictate my dating choices.	☐
I feel emotionally available and ready to receive love.	☐
I don't expect others to guess what I need, I can express it.	☐
I value healthy boundaries and can honor them in others.	☐

Reflection: In what ways can you continue growing emotionally?

SECTION 4: Lifestyle & Purpose Compatibility

Statement	Rating
I have personal goals and purpose that I'm actively working toward.	☐
I understand what I bring to a relationship, spiritually, emotionally, and practically.	☐
I am financially and mentally responsible for myself.	☐
I know the difference between partnership and dependency.	☐
I am open to adjusting for the right connection, but not at the cost of losing myself.	☐

Reflection: How do your lifestyle and values prepare you for partnership?

Final Thoughts:

Total Score: _____ / 100

- **85–100** → You're deeply grounded and emotionally ready for a relationship rooted in purpose and peace.
- **65–84** → You're on the right track, keep building awareness, healing, and alignment.
- **Below 65** → Take time to intentionally prepare. Healing, clarity, and wholeness will make future connection more fulfilling.

Prayer of Preparation:

Lord, prepare my heart for divine connection.

Heal the places in me that still carry fear, disappointment, or residue from the past.

Help me to see myself the way You see me, worthy of love, respect, and joy.

Align my desires with Your will.

Make me ready for the person who will sharpen, support, and walk beside me in purpose.

Until then, grow me in wisdom, grace, and self-awareness.

In Jesus' name, amen.

Chapter Eighteen:

"WHEN THE STRONG FEEL STRAINED"

Question:

What are effective ways to cope with a partner's mental health issues?

Our Story:

We both hit a wall, but not at the same time.

One of us was still moving forward in ministry, smiling through every responsibility. The other was fading behind the scenes, quietly unraveling under the weight of anxiety, fatigue, and unspoken fears.

We were praying. We were still serving. But we were both quietly worn down, spiritually rich but emotionally drained.

There were moments we didn't know what to say to each other. Times where one of us felt helpless… and the other felt hopeless. But what carried us wasn't perfection. It was presence. Patience. And the decision to stay connected, even when the emotions didn't always make sense.

We learned that spiritual maturity doesn't make you immune to mental struggle. It just gives you an anchor while you face it.

He Says:

I was the one who hit the wall first.

It started with overworking, then withdrawing. I wasn't trying to shut her out, I just didn't have the language for what I was feeling. The pressure, the fatigue, the quiet frustration. It felt easier to just go silent.

But she didn't let me stay in that place.

She didn't push. She didn't panic. She just kept showing up. She prayed with me. Sat near me. And asked, "How's your heart today?" even when she didn't get a deep answer.

Here's what helped me:

Permission to not be okay. I didn't need to perform my way back to strength. I needed space to feel without shame.

Spiritual covering, not spiritual pressure. She didn't throw verses at me. She just reminded me God was still close, and so was she.

Small check-ins that felt safe. A hug. A shared devotional. A gentle, "Let's take a walk." It meant more than I could say.

Men, if you're struggling mentally or emotionally, you are not weak. You are human. And you are loved.

Let your spouse in. Let God in. And remember: you can be both spiritual and seeking help.

She Says:

Burnout snuck up on me like a fog.

I didn't lose my faith. I didn't stop believing God's promises. But I felt numb, emotionally worn down and spiritually dry.

He saw it before I could admit it.

And instead of criticizing, he covered me. He prayed for me when I didn't have the strength to pray for myself. He took on extra responsibilities to give me breathing room. He asked questions with compassion, not control.

Love Has to Be Stronger Than Words Supporting someone through mental or emotional strain takes more than advice, it takes *presence.* It's one thing to quote scriptures and send encouragement. It's another thing to **sit in the silence**, show up when the energy is gone, and hold space when answers don't come easily.

We've both had seasons, yes, both, where the weight of life, ministry, responsibility, and silent battles took a toll. We didn't always see it coming. And we didn't always know how to talk about it.
But we knew we wanted to fight *with* each other, not *against* the invisible pressures we both were facing.

Here's what helped us both:

Normalize the Need for Rest. Ministry burnout is real. And for a long time, we wore it like a badge of honor. No days off. No breaks. No boundaries. Just doing "the Lord's work" while secretly unraveling inside. But eventually, God made it clear: **He never asked us to sacrifice our sanity for service.**

We had to stop spiritualizing overwork.
We had to stop acting like being tired was a sign of faithfulness.
And we had to learn how to *Sabbath on purpose.*
We started carving out space, not just for sleep, but for recovery. For laughter. For non-church-related fun. For stillness. Because rest doesn't make you lazy, it makes you *last.*

Encourage Professional Help. We're prayer warriors, but we're also **pro-therapy**. We believe in laying hands, but we also believe in laying on a licensed therapist's couch when needed. Healing isn't limited to the altar, sometimes it happens in the therapist's chair.

There were times when prayer gave us peace, but counseling gave us *tools.* Times when we needed a safe space to unpack things that didn't have quick spiritual answers. We sought out Christian counselors who understood both *faith and mental health*, and it made all the difference.
Getting help doesn't mean you're broken. It means you're **brave enough to get better**.

Presence Over Pressure. When one of us was mentally or emotionally drained, the other had to learn not to fix, but to *stand close.* We didn't always need a solution. Sometimes we just needed each other. We learned to ask: "What do you need right now?"
And when words weren't enough, we let hugs, quiet, and prayer do the talking.

Practice Soul-Care, Not Just Self-Care. We've learned there's a big difference between *self-care* and *soul-care.* Self-care is important, yes. It's the bubble baths, the naps, the spa days, the walks around the block to clear your head.

But **soul-care goes deeper.** It's about checking the condition of your spirit, your mind, and your emotional reserves. It's making space for your soul to breathe, to rest, to process, to reconnect with God and with each other.

We started doing simple things that fed our souls, not just our schedules. We took walks. Not to power-walk through problems, but to *pause and be present* with each other. We took breaks from ministry, not because we didn't love it, but because we needed time to remember why we were called in the first place. We took time off to just be, not to produce, not to plan, but to just *exist in peace.*

Soul-care meant we prayed together and played together. We watched sunsets without a sermon. We sat in silence without pressure to "talk it out." We revisited our joy. Our laughter. Our rhythm as a couple outside of roles and responsibilities.

And what we found was that when the soul is nourished, the heart becomes lighter, and connection becomes easier. Now, we make soul-care a priority. Not just when we're running on empty, but as a rhythm of rest, **so we never forget that God didn't just create us to do, He created us to dwell.**

One verse that held me was Psalm 34:18 – "The Lord is close to the brokenhearted and saves those who are crushed in spirit."

To any couple walking through emotional exhaustion, burnout, or mental health strain: **Don't ignore it. Don't hide it. And don't try to carry it alone.**

Love isn't loud, it's consistent.
Faith isn't fake, it's full of compassion.
And healing doesn't always come quickly, but it *does come* when you create space for it.

If you're the one supporting your spouse:
You don't have to have all the answers. You just have to be there.

If you're the one struggling:
You're not a burden. You're not broken. You're brave, for choosing to face it.

We Say:

Faith, Feelings, and Finding Help

As pastors, we've witnessed the transformative power of prayer, but we've also seen the damage that silence, shame, and spiritual bypassing can do when mental health challenges are swept under the rug in the name of "being strong" or "just having more faith."

Here's what we've come to believe with conviction:
God is not intimidated by our emotions, nor is He absent in our therapy sessions.

We firmly stand in the truth that **faith and mental wellness go hand-in-hand**. Seeking help, from a counselor, therapist, doctor, or support group, does not contradict your belief in God's healing power. In fact, it honors it. Why? Because God can work through people. He uses the oil *and* the hands. He anoints the prayer *and* the plan.

When one spouse is struggling mentally or emotionally, both feel it. It's not just a personal issue, it becomes a relational one. But the good news is: **you're not powerless**. You can support without enabling. You can pray without pretending. You can seek help without guilt. And you can grow stronger, even through the darkness.

We encourage couples to:

- **Talk to each other honestly** about what's hard, even if it's awkward.
- **Set boundaries** around triggers and unhealthy cycles.
- **Invite Jesus into the process** of counseling, medication (if needed), therapy, and spiritual growth.
- **Remember that healing is a journey, not just a moment.**

Let this be your takeaway:
It's not unspiritual to ask for help. It's unwise not to.
And if Christ carried a cross for your healing, don't carry unnecessary shame that keeps you from receiving it.
You are not broken beyond repair.
You are not alone in the process.
And you don't have to choose between your Bible and your breakthrough.

Choose both.
, *With compassion and conviction*

Stress & Burnout Red Flags Checklist

"You can't pour from an empty vessel. Pay attention before breakdown becomes burnout."

Foundational Scripture:

Matthew 11:28 (AMP)

"Come to Me, all who are weary and heavily burdened [by religious rituals that provide no peace], and I will give you rest [refreshing your souls with salvation]."

Mental & Emotional Warning Signs

☐ Trouble concentrating or making decisions

☐ Irritability or constant frustration over small things

☐ Frequent mood swings or emotional numbness

☐ Anxiety that seems to come from nowhere

☐ Feeling overwhelmed even by routine tasks

☐ Persistent feelings of guilt, shame, or failure

☐ Lack of motivation or decreased sense of joy

Physical Warning Signs

- ☐ Chronic fatigue (even after sleep)
- ☐ Headaches, body aches, or unexplained pain
- ☐ Changes in appetite (eating too much or too little)
- ☐ Insomnia or disrupted sleep patterns
- ☐ Increased heart rate or frequent tension in the body
- ☐ Digestive issues or frequent illness

Relational & Spiritual Warning Signs

- ☐ Withdrawing from loved ones or avoiding conversations
- ☐ Becoming overly defensive or emotionally distant
- ☐ Loss of patience with spouse, children, or co-workers
- ☐ Lack of desire to pray, worship, or engage spiritually

- ☐ Going through the motions spiritually but feeling disconnected
- ☐ Feeling resentment toward God, the church, or responsibilities
- ☐ Saying "yes" out of guilt, not grace

Lifestyle & Work Pattern Red Flags

- ☐ Working non-stop or struggling to "turn off" at the end of the day
- ☐ Constant multitasking but feeling like nothing is fully done
- ☐ Overcommitting and under-resting
- ☐ Neglecting hobbies or things that once brought joy
- ☐ Ignoring personal goals or vision due to survival mode
- ☐ Feeling stuck in performance instead of purpose

What to Do If You Checked 5 or More Boxes

- **Pause:** Make time to acknowledge what your body, mind, and spirit are telling you.
- **Pray:** Ask God to reveal the root of your exhaustion and give you the grace to shift.
- **Prioritize:** Reevaluate your commitments, what's urgent vs. what's eternal?
- **Partner:** Talk to your spouse, pastor, a counselor, mentor, or trusted friend.
- **Protect:** Set boundaries that preserve your peace and restore your soul.
- **Practice rest:** Not just sleep, but soul-level stillness. (Psalm 23:3 – "He restores my soul…")

Prayer for Renewal

Lord, show me where I'm running on empty.
Teach me how to rest without guilt and say no without fear.
Restore the joy that fatigue has stolen, and help me hear You again in the stillness.

I release the pressure to perform, and I receive Your invitation to simply be.
Refresh my soul, renew my mind, and remind my heart that I don't have to carry this alone.
In Jesus' name, amen.

Mental Health Support Map for Couples

Step 1: Begin With a Grounding Prayer
"God, thank You for not leaving us alone in hard seasons. Teach us to be safe places for each other. Remind us that healing is holy, and progress, no matter how small, is still progress. Lead us with grace and peace."

Step 2: Recognize the Signs of Struggle
As a couple, reflect gently, no blame, no shame.

Check any that apply to either of you:

- Unexplained fatigue, burnout, or emotional numbness
- Increased irritability or emotional distance
- Withdrawing from spiritual practices or social connection
- Feeling overwhelmed or anxious for extended periods
- Difficulty concentrating or sleeping
- Loss of interest in activities that once brought joy

If several apply, this is a signal to slow down, talk, and take steps toward support.

Step 3: Create a "Safe Talk" Space
Use this structure to check in without judgment:

- "What's been weighing on you this week?"
- "What kind of support feels helpful right now, listening, prayer, space, or action?"
- "Do you want comfort, solutions, or just quiet presence?"
- "How are we doing spiritually, individually and together?"

Set a weekly rhythm for this, short, consistent, and sacred.

Step 4: Build Your Support Toolkit
Discuss and list what's available and needed.

Support Source	Do We Have This?	Need to Add?
Personal prayer time	Y/ N	Y/ N
Couple prayer time	Y/ N	Y/ N
Trusted friends/mentors	Y/ N	Y/ N
Licensed therapist/counselor	Y/ N	Y/ N
Rest days/Sabbath time	Y/ N	Y/ N
Creative release (journaling, music, etc.)	Y/ N	Y/ N

Step 5: Set Boundaries With Love

Identify things that help and hurt the healing process:

- "What conversations or activities feel too heavy right now?"
- "What boundaries can we put in place to protect peace this week?"
- "What can we pause or delegate to reduce pressure?"

Remember: Boundaries protect both healing and connection.

Step 6: Reaffirm Your Partnership

End each check-in with this declaration:

"We are not fighting each other, we are fighting for each other. We are not alone. We are growing, healing, and walking in grace. One day at a time. Together."

Scriptures for Strength & Healing

- **Psalm 34:18** – "The Lord is close to the brokenhearted…"
- **Matthew 11:28** – "Come to Me, all who are weary… I will give you rest."
- **Isaiah 40:29** – "He gives strength to the weary…"
- **Ecclesiastes 4:10** – "If one falls, the other can help them up."

Chapter Nineteen:

"INTIMACY ISN'T ALWAYS INSTANT"

Question:

How do we maintain a healthy sexual relationship in marriage?

Our Story:

Let's be real, we are not your "typical" couple when it comes to intimacy.

I am the passionate one. Always ready to connect physically, emotionally, spiritually.

He loves intimacy too, but when stress piles up (and it has), his desire takes a back seat.

We've lived through:
Financial setbacks
Ministry burnout
Moments where the mind was full and the body was… just tired

In those seasons, our rhythms didn't match, and it caused tension.

Not because we didn't love each other, but because we weren't on the same page in the same season.

What we learned? Sex isn't just about physical need, it's about emotional availability, spiritual peace, and intentional communication.

He Says:

Listen, if you had told me early in our marriage that I'd be the one saying *"not tonight"* more often than my wife, I would've laughed.

But real talk? It happened.
And it caught *both* of us off guard.

It wasn't about attraction, she's fine, saved, and mine.
It wasn't about desire, she turns my head in every room.
But life was… *a lot.*

Between ministry, job loss, financial pressure, trying to be everything to everybody, I was worn out. Not just tired, **empty**. And when your soul is running on fumes, intimacy can start to feel like one more thing on the list instead of the joy it's supposed to be.

And the worst part?
I knew she noticed.
I saw it in her eyes.
The wondering. The waiting. The "am I too much?" that she never said, but I felt. And man, that hit me hard.

Because I never wanted her to feel rejected. But the truth is, **sometimes we don't talk about how stress can sabotage desire.**
It's not that I didn't want her. I just didn't have much left to give.
I was trying to survive, and she was trying to connect, and somewhere in between, the intimacy got lost.

But here's what helped us reclaim that space:
She didn't stop pursuing me, but she stopped pressuring me.
She started approaching intimacy as an *invitation*, not a demand.
That made all the difference. It reminded me that this wasn't about performance, it was about *presence.*

We talked about it, like, really talked. I opened up about my stress. She opened up about her desire. And somewhere in that vulnerability, we found our rhythm again. She let me be honest without shame, and I let her be passionate without apology.

We realized intimacy isn't one-size-fits-all. Some nights, passion looked like long kisses and laughter. Other nights, it looked like prayer, a shoulder rub, and falling asleep mid-conversation. And sometimes? It was just *knowing we were still on the same team*, even if our bodies weren't always synced up.

Now? We're in a better place.
Not perfect, but **connected**.
We check in. We play. We flirt. We prioritize intimacy, physically *and* emotionally.
Because we've learned that passion isn't about pressure, it's about presence, patience, and *partnership*.

To my brothers:
If you're feeling overwhelmed, tired, or like your desire's been dimmed, **you're not broken.** You're human. But don't suffer in silence. Talk about it. Pray about it. Let your wife *see you*, not just physically, but *fully*.

And to my sisters:
If your passion burns hotter, don't tone it down. Bring it with love, with invitation, and with joy. **God isn't afraid of your fire, He *designed* it for covenant.** And trust me, when we honor each other's differences without shame, **intimacy becomes not just sacred... but *scorching*.**

She Says:

Desire Isn't Shameful, It's Sacred. I know it's not "typical" by most people's standards, but let's be real, I'm the one in our marriage with the higher sex drive.

Yes, I love Jesus.
Yes, I love ministry.
Yes, I also love *physical closeness*, connection, and all the fire that comes with covenant.

But in the beginning, when our rhythms were off, I struggled.
I started questioning everything:
"Is he not attracted to me?"
"Am I being too much?"
"Why do I feel like I'm chasing what's supposed to be ours?"

There were nights I felt rejected. Days I felt confused. And because intimacy is such a vulnerable place for a woman, it wasn't just about sex. It was about feeling wanted. *Seen. Desired. Chosen.*

And when that wasn't happening in the way I expected, the silence echoed louder than words. But over time, I realized, **he wasn't rejecting me. He was *surviving something*.**

Life. Stress. Financial strain. Ministry pressure. Expectations. Internal weight he didn't always have the language to unpack. And when I finally paused and chose to look past my frustration and into his *heart*,

I found something I didn't expect: **Compassion.**

Here's what helped us grow through it, not just as lovers, but as partners:

Open, unfiltered conversations. I didn't mask my desire with silence or sarcasm. I spoke it, gently, but clearly. And he shared his emotional exhaustion without shame. That honesty became a bridge, not a battlefield.

I learned to initiate without demanding. Let's be clear, there's nothing wrong with a wife initiating intimacy. But there's a difference between invitation and *insistence.* So I shifted my tone, my timing, and my posture. Instead of making it a performance metric, I made it an *offering.* And when he saw that I wasn't pressuring him, but *pursuing him in love*, everything shifted.

We built intimacy beyond the bedroom. Sometimes it was flirty texts that said, "I'm thinking about you." Other times it was soft touches in passing, or long looks that said, "I still choose you."
We prayed together, cooked together, and *laughed until we felt like us again.* That emotional closeness made physical intimacy deeper, more meaningful, more intentional, more *fire.* Because real passion isn't always about frequency. Sometimes, it's about depth.

The verse I held onto in that season, and still do, is **Song of Solomon 7:10**: *"I belong to my beloved, and his desire is for me."* That's not just poetic, it's prophetic. It reminded me that even when desire *looks* different, our covenant is still secure. We're not always on the same schedule, but we're always on the same side.

My sisters with strong desire:
You are not too much. Your passion is not shameful, it's sacred.
And to my brothers navigating pressure, fatigue, or performance anxiety:
You are not broken. You are human. And you are loved.
God created intimacy for covenant, not comparison. And when we love each other through desire differences, with honesty, playfulness, patience, and prayer, *it gets better, richer, and more deeply fulfilling over time.*

Don't be afraid to explore each other, spiritually and physically. The marriage bed is blessed (Hebrews 13:4). And intimacy, when nurtured in love and led by God, isn't just good, it's *glory-filled.*

We Say:

Desire & Connection Reset Exercise

Step 1: Center the Moment in Prayer
Before you begin, hold hands and invite God in:

"Lord, thank You for the gift of intimacy. Help us speak with honesty, listen with grace, and grow in trust. Help us see each other's hearts, not just our differences. We desire closeness, emotionally, spiritually, and physically. Be in the center of it all."

Step 2: Check In, Without Judgment
Each partner takes a few minutes to answer the following:

Partner 1:
Lately, I've felt closest to you when:
➤ ____

One thing I've longed for more of (emotionally or physically):
➤ ____

One thing that's been affecting my desire or energy:
➤ ____

Partner 2:
Lately, I've felt most connected when:
➤ ____

Something I need to feel emotionally safe and open:
➤ ____

A pressure I've been carrying (mentally, spiritually, or physically):

➤ ____

Important: Let your partner share fully before responding. This moment is about understanding, not fixing.

Step 3: Reconnect With Intention
Now explore together:

What kind of intimacy do we need most this week?

- ➤ [ ] Physical closeness
- ➤ [ ] Deep conversation
- ➤ [ ] Spiritual unity
- ➤ [ ] Fun and laughter
- ➤ [ ] A break from pressure
- ➤ [ ] Something else: ______________

What's one small thing we can do to reconnect this week?
➤ ____

Ideas:

- Light candles and share a meal at home
- Take a no-phones walk
- Cuddle with no expectations
- Share one thing you love about each other, every day for a week
- Schedule intimacy and talk about it beforehand

Step 4: Reflect on Truth Together

- **1 Corinthians 7:3–4** – "The husband should fulfill his marital duty to his wife, and likewise the wife to her husband… their bodies belong to each other."
- **Proverbs 5:18–19** – "May you rejoice in the wife of your youth… may you ever be intoxicated with her love."

Remember:

- Intimacy is more than physical, it's emotional, spiritual, and relational.
- Desire can ebb and flow, but covenant remains.
- You're not failing. You're growing. Together.

Closing Statement (Say it together):
"We are one. We are learning each other in every season. Our connection is worth protecting, nurturing, and enjoying. We will keep showing up, with grace, without pressure, and always in love."

~ This is so important we are giving you two couple's activities ~

His & Her Intimacy Journal Prompts
"And the two shall become one...", Mark 10:8

For Him: Reflecting on Desire, Connection & Emotional Availability

1. What does intimacy mean to me beyond sex? How do I best give and receive affection?
2. Are there moments when I've felt disconnected from my wife emotionally or physically? Why?
3. What helps me feel most desired and confident in our relationship?
4. When I'm stressed or emotionally withdrawn, how do I want to be approached or supported?
5. Have I clearly communicated my physical and emotional needs? If not, what's been the barrier?
6. What spiritual practices (prayer, rest, worship) help me reconnect with my sense of intimacy and identity as a husband?
7. What's one way I can be more intentional in expressing desire, verbally or nonverbally, this week?

For Her: Reflecting on Desire, Safety & Vulnerability

1. How do I define intimacy, and what role does emotional connection play in physical desire for me?
2. Have I ever internalized unmet desire as rejection? What did I need in those moments?
3. In what ways do I express desire toward my husband, and what might make that expression feel more honoring for both of us?
4. How do I balance vulnerability with understanding when our rhythms are off?
5. What insecurities do I need to surrender to God when it comes to my body, needs, or expectations?
6. What spiritual affirmations help me stay rooted in the truth that desire is sacred, not shameful?
7. What's one way I can create a space for intimacy this week, not just physically, but emotionally or spiritually?

Together Reflection Prompts

1. What has been one of our best moments of intimacy, and what made it special?
2. Where do we feel most disconnected right now, and how can we close the gap together?
3. What helps us both feel seen, safe, and wanted? Are we practicing those things consistently?
4. Have we prayed together about our intimate life? If not, what's stopping us?
5. What boundaries, habits, or distractions might be interrupting deeper intimacy, and are we ready to release them?
6. How can we continue to prioritize passion in a way that reflects both our personalities and our purpose?
7. What does God want to teach us about intimacy in this season of our marriage?

Suggested Use:

- Choose 1–2 prompts each week.
- Journal individually, then share with one another during a set time (e.g., date night, weekend wind-down).

- End your time with a **prayer together**, thanking God for your covenant and inviting Him to continue maturing your love.

Chapter Twenty:

"STILL US, EVEN WITH THEM"

Question:

How can we keep our relationship strong after having children?

Our Story:

By the time we got married, our children were older. Some were out of the house, some were close. We didn't raise babies together, and we didn't walk through midnight feedings or toddler tantrums as a team.

But we have sat across the table from couples who did, and who are now asking the same question:

"How do we keep this love strong when we're exhausted, distracted, and always tending to someone else?"

While we didn't parent babies side-by-side, we've mentored couples through:

The newborn fog that made them feel more like roommates than lovers

The jealousy that came when one partner felt neglected

The identity shift that made it hard to prioritize romance

The guilt of wanting "us time" in the middle of raising kids

We've witnessed one truth over and over again:

Children thrive when they see love between their parents, and that love must be protected, pursued, and prioritized.

He Says:

One thing I always tell younger husbands is this:
Your wife didn't stop needing you just because the baby arrived.

The demands may have changed, but her heart still needs your attention, your presence, and your tenderness.

Yes, it's hard to balance it all. Sleepless nights, long work days, crying babies. But don't let the needs of parenting erase the call to be a partner.

What I've encouraged men to do:

Keep dating your wife, even if it's in the living room. Intention matters more than expense.

Communicate about exhaustion and roles. Don't assume she's okay. Don't assume you are, either. Talk about it.

Ask how she's really doing, not just as a mom, but as a woman. Listen. And affirm her deeply.

If she is a stay home Mom, give her time to herself. You are not "babysitting," you are being a Father.

And spiritually, remember:
Children are a gift, not a replacement. Proverbs 5:18–19 reminds us to "rejoice in the wife of your youth." That's not just a honeymoon verse, it's a lifelong reminder.

Brother, don't stop pursuing her. Your love isn't just a blessing to her, it's a model for your children.

She Says:

I've watched so many amazing women go from being seen as beautiful partners to feeling like they've become invisible after baby.

Motherhood is beautiful, but it's consuming. And if you're not careful, it can pull your marriage into the background. Not because you don't love each other, but because everything is loud, urgent, and exhausting.

When I talk to wives and young moms, I remind them:

Your need for love, affection, and intimacy doesn't make you selfish. It makes you human.

You don't stop being a wife because you became a mother. Both roles matter. And you're allowed to want more than diapers and dishes.

Ask for what you need. Don't assume your spouse can see the burnout on your face. Speak up, with love, not resentment.

Together, you can:

Schedule 15-minute "check-in" moments, even with a baby monitor nearby.

Plan monthly "marriage nights" after bedtime (candles, music – use Marvin Gaye not Marvin Sapp, real conversation).

When he offers to give you time to yourself, take it! He may not do things the way that you would but he is not you. If you try to control everything, you will find yourself doing everything with only yourself to blame.

Pray over your relationship, not just your children. Invite your husband to pray over you as he gently touches you.

The verse that I recommend is Matthew 19:6 – "What God has joined together, let no one separate." That includes the busyness of parenting. That includes the good intentions that lead to disconnection. Your marriage is holy ground. Guard it with grace.

We Say:

Love Beyond the Baby Phase: A Connection Planning Guide

Step 1: Pray for Unity, Energy & Intimacy

"Lord, thank You for the gift of our children and the calling to love one another well. Teach us to care for each other in the chaos. Help us protect our marriage with intention, even when our schedules feel full. Reignite passion, restore energy, and give us joy as we grow in love and parenthood, together."

Step 2: Quick Connection Check-In

Each of you answers these prompts honestly, gently, and without interruption:

- "One thing that's helped me feel close to you recently is…"
- "One thing that's been draining me emotionally or physically is…"
- "I would feel more supported if…"
- "I miss when we used to…"

"Right now, I need more (choose one or more):"

- [ ] Quality time
- [ ] Words of affirmation
- [ ] Physical intimacy
- [ ] Laughter and fun
- [ ] Spiritual connection
- [ ] Rest and space

Step 3: The "Us Time" Strategy (Weekly, Monthly, Daily)

Use these three rhythms to protect your relationship in a full season.

Daily Connection (5–15 minutes)

Idea	*Frequency*	*Who's Leading?*
Eye contact and check-in: "How's your heart?"	Daily	________
Hugs/kisses with no agenda	Daily	________
Whispered prayer before bed or before work	Daily	________

Weekly Connection (30–90 minutes)

Idea	*Day of Week*	*Details*
After-kid-bedtime "date"	__________	Movie, snacks, music, no phones
Intimacy reset time	__________	Talk + touch + no guilt expectations
Shared devotional or journal prompt	__________	Use your Real, Relevant, and Raw prayer book

Monthly Connection (2–4 hours)

Idea	*Planned Date*	*Notes*
Babysitter + date night	__________	Keep it light, fun, romantic
Marriage check-in session	__________	Goals, prayers, challenges, affirmations
Overnight getaway or day retreat (quarterly)	__________	Even if it's local or in-home

Step 4: Reality Check + Grace Plan

Discuss:

- What's realistic for us right now?
- Where have we let survival mode become the standard?

- How can we give each other grace, but also gently call each other back to connection?

Remember: One skipped date night doesn't break a bond. But many weeks of unspoken disconnection can. Reconnect now. Often. Gently.

Scriptures to Anchor This Season

- **Matthew 19:6** – "What God has joined together, let no one separate."
- **Ecclesiastes 9:9** – "Enjoy life with your wife, whom you love…"
- **Proverbs 5:18** – "May you rejoice in the wife of your youth."
- **Galatians 6:9** – "Let us not become weary in doing good…"

Closing Declaration

Say this together:

"We are more than parents, we are partners. We choose connection over convenience, presence over pressure, and intimacy over assumption. Our love is not paused, it's being refined. We're still growing. Still pursuing. Still choosing each other, on purpose."

Chapter Twenty-One:

"WE ALMOST WALKED AWAY"

Question:

What should we do if we're considering separating or divorcing?

Our Story:

This chapter isn't easy to write, but it's necessary. There was a season where things got really hard. Not between us emotionally, but around us financially. Bills stacked up. Income slowed down. We were trying everything, working long hours, cutting back, praying hard, but the weight wouldn't lift. We were still praying together. Still saying "I love you." But under the surface, shame started speaking. One night, through tears, one of us said: "You'd probably be better off without me. I'm just holding you back." The other responded, "If you walk away, I won't be free. I'll be broken."

That conversation revealed a heartbreaking dilemma: not that we didn't love each other, but that our love for each other was now being tested by our desire not to become a burden. The fear was not merely about lack of funds, but that continuing to struggle together might somehow limit the other's potential happiness or success. This fear nearly shattered the foundation of our marriage, not because we lacked love, but because we cared deeply about each other's wellbeing.

Things between us had reached a critical point. The financial strain and emotional stress began to erode our confidence in our shared future. Even our commitments within the ministry began to feel the impact, as our personal turmoil bled into every effort and interaction, haunting us with doubt and fear about our collective calling.

We were still praying together. Still saying "I love you."
But under the surface, shame started speaking.

One night, through tears, one of us said:

"You'd probably be better off without me. I'm just holding you back."

The other responded,

"If you walk away, I won't be free. I'll be broken."

That moment exposed the quiet fear: not that we didn't love each other, but that love wasn't enough to carry the weight of our struggle.

Amidst the swirling storm of our financial woes, our ministry also began to flounder. We poured our hearts into the community, served tirelessly, and did everything we could to be light in the darkness, but it often felt like our efforts disappeared into a void. Attendance at events dwindled. Criticism, both external and from within our group, seeped into conversations.

Each failed initiative added layers to the heartache. Our outreach programs, once vibrant and impactful, now struggled to make even the smallest ripple. We knew the community's needs had not diminished; if anything, they were more pressing than ever. Yet, our ability to serve effectively seemed crippled by an invisible barrier, frustration wearing down our spirits day after dreary day.

In the quiet, candid moments we found together amidst the chaos, we questioned everything. "Are we still doing His work?" one would ask. "Is our faith not strong enough?" the other might reply late at night, voices low but heavy with aching confusion and grief. This doubt, the feeling of heavenly silence, cast long shadows over what had once been a shared journey lit by surety and divine purpose.

In seeking clarity, we pressed deeper into prayer, our pleas fervent for guidance or even the slightest affirmation that our struggles weren't in vain. It was in these moments of vulnerability, between sobs and supplications, that we found not answers, perhaps, but a strengthening of our bond, a reinforcement of our unity under God's gaze, even if the path remained obscured by shadows.

One particularly testing evening, the heavens seemed to open slightly, offering us a sliver of understanding. We were in the middle of discussing yet another cancelled program when suddenly, through the simple yet profound act of mutual consolation, a realization crystallized between us: our ministry, though it seemed in ruins, was not the sole measure of our calling or success. Indeed, failure in the eyes of the world did not equate to failure in the eyes of God. Perhaps, we pondered, our true ministry was not to succeed always but to remain steadfast in faith, to embody resilience, and to reflect His grace through our unyielding commitment to each other and to our shared vocation.

Thus, armed with redefined purpose and a refreshing perspective, we agreed that though the journey was fraught with trials, our resolve would not falter. We would count every small victory, every fleeting moment of joy and communion, as profound success. Our love, our marriage, and our shared faith would be our ministry, as powerful and poignant in failure as it was in triumph.

And perhaps, this was the lesson intended for us all along: that God's workings are most potent in our weaknesses, most evident in our unity, and most triumphant in our persevering heart. Grace, indeed, was the answer, not merely as a remedy for shame but as a foundational principle guiding us through unrecognized victories in our journey together. We didn't need space from each other. We needed a deeper understanding of how God was still working in the dark.

He Says:

I didn't want to leave her.
I wanted to free her.

At least, that's what I told myself.

We were going through so much financially. I felt like a failure as a provider. I watched her work, sacrifice, encourage me, and still smile. And deep down, I thought, "She deserves more than this. More than me."

That kind of thinking doesn't come from God. It comes from unhealed shame.

What I learned through that season:

My value isn't in what I produce. It's in who I am in Christ, and in this marriage.

Being broke doesn't mean I'm broken. And loving someone in hard times means staying, not saving face.

I had to talk, not hide. My silence almost created a wedge that love didn't deserve.

Romans 8:1 says, "There is no condemnation for those who are in Christ Jesus."

That includes me. That includes you. That includes us.

If you're thinking of leaving because you feel like a burden, don't. Your spouse chose you for all seasons. Let love speak louder than fear.

She Says:

I saw the weight on him before he said a word, so much weight, but I knew it wasn't his alone.

The pressure. The pain. The way his shoulders slumped when the bills came in. The way my confidence in myself, in us, seemed to fade with every reminder of our ministry's failure.

He still loved me deeply, but in that season, neither of us knew how to love ourselves. And it wasn't just him who thought I'd be better off without him. I wrestled with the same thoughts, that maybe he'd be better off without me. That the shame I carried, the guilt of everything falling apart, was too much to ask him to bear.

When he shared how he felt, when he confessed that he thought I'd be better off without him, it broke me. But it didn't surprise me, because it was the mirror of my own fears. Somehow, we'd started believing the same lie: that our failures defined us, and our love wasn't enough to hold us together.

But here's what I've learned, and what I've clung to, even through all the shame:

When love still exists, don't let lies make your decisions for you.

Shame distorts everything it touches. That voice that whispers, "You're not enough," that screams, "You're better off alone", it isn't truth, and it isn't God. It's fear. It's the weight of broken dreams and unfinished hopes trying to drown you.

But love is worth fighting for. Even if you feel crushed by failure, even if the shame is telling you to walk away, if love is still present, fight. Together. Not against each other, but for each other. For everything you believe in, and everything God has promised.

We didn't fight alone. It started with a decision, a shift, from praying separately in our own private spaces to coming together nightly in a shared prayer space. We chose to face the weight of our pain, our failures, and our shame as one. Together, we lifted up our brokenness to God, prayed fervently for healing, cried for strength, and sought peace as a team. It wasn't always easy, but those moments of shared vulnerability became the foundation for our fight. We battled through the remnants of our failures, adjusted our budget, compromised, and rebuilt our peace one choosing-faith moment at a time.

And God, faithful as He always is, showed up. Even when we felt crushed, He was near. Even when shame whispered that we were alone, He reminded us we never were.

Psalm 34:18 says it perfectly: "The Lord is close to the brokenhearted." We were brokenhearted. In truth, we were shattered. But brokenness doesn't scare God, it draws Him near. And in Him, we found the strength to stay. To fight. To rebuild. Together.

We Say:

What We Recommend If You're Considering Separation:

Pause and Pray, Together.
Don't make permanent decisions from a temporary storm.

Talk It Out, With Compassion.
Ask: "Is this about us… or about the pressure we're under?"
"Are we afraid we're failing, or just tired of fighting alone?"

Seek Wise, Godly Counsel.
A trusted pastor, counselor, or mentor couple can speak life into your situation. You don't have to figure it out alone.

Name the Real Enemy.
Financial stress. Mental health. Past trauma. Outside expectations. These may be the root, not each other.

Remember Your Vows.
You said "for better or worse." This might be the "worse", but worse doesn't mean worthless.

Stay, Heal, Rebuild: A Courageous Plan for Couples in Crisis
For couples who still love each other, but are questioning if they can keep going. This guide helps you pause, process, and pursue healing, together.

Step 1: Pause and Pray
Before you do anything else, stop and invite God in.

Hold hands, sit quietly, or journal this simple prayer:
"Lord, we are tired. We are hurting. But we still care. Show us what's worth fighting for. Help us hear each other clearly and love each

other deeply. We don't want to run. We want to rebuild. Even if we don't know how, help us start."

Step 2: Start an Honest Conversation

Use these prompts to check in:

- "What's really causing this feeling of wanting to give up?"
- "Do you feel unloved, unseen, or like a burden?"
- "What lies have you started to believe about yourself, or about me?"
- "Are we experiencing a relationship problem… or a life pressure problem?"

Important: Don't try to fix it all today. Just speak, listen, and breathe.

Step 3: Identify What Needs Healing

Together or individually, complete the sentence:

- "I think I need healing in the area of ________."
- "I've been hurting because ________."
- "I've been carrying ________ and it's been too heavy alone."

Often, it's shame, fear, exhaustion, or unmet expectations that need to be named, so healing can begin.

Step 4: Ask for Help, Together

Choose 1–2 safe people or resources who can walk with you:

- Pastor or spiritual mentor
- Licensed Christian counselor
- Trusted married couple who has been through hardship
- Financial coach or advisor (if money is the root issue)

Proverbs 11:14 – "In the multitude of counselors there is safety."

Step 5: Rebuild Your Foundation, One Brick at a Time

Start small. Don't rush. Rebuilding takes time.

Pick 3 areas to start with:

Area	Our First Step
Emotional Closeness	________________
Communication	________________
Financial Peace	________________
Intimacy	________________
Shared Time	________________
Spiritual Connection	________________

Example: "Let's do a 10-minute check-in every night this week" or "Let's fast and pray together every Wednesday."

Scriptures for This Season

- **Romans 8:1** – "There is no condemnation for those who are in Christ…"
- **Isaiah 43:2** – "When you pass through the waters, I will be with you…"
- **Psalm 147:3** – "He heals the brokenhearted and binds up their wounds."
- **1 Peter 5:10** – "After you have suffered a little while… He will restore you."

Closing Declaration (Say Together):

"We are not done. We are not beyond repair. We are still chosen, for each other, and by God. We will walk through this pain, not around it. And with God's help, we will rebuild something deeper than before. One step, one prayer, one day at a time."

Chapter Twenty-Two:

"LET'S TURN THE LIGHTS BACK ON"

Question:

What should we do if our sex life has become stale or unfulfilling?

Our Story:

We never lost love. We didn't stop finding each other attractive. But there came a stretch where our sex life got… well, routine.

The passion was still there, but hidden under layers of work stress, physical fatigue, emotional disconnection, and differing libidos. She had the higher sex drive, while he felt worn down by the demands of daily life. We started missing each other, not just in the bedroom, but in rhythm, timing, and expectation.

There was no infidelity. No moral failure. Just distance… silence… and a creeping fear that "maybe this is just how marriage gets after a while." But we weren't ready to settle for function over fire.

So, we prayed. We talked deeply about our feelings, our desires, and our needs. We decided not to just hope for change but to actively pursue it.

We acknowledged that intimacy is multifaceted, it's not just physical but also emotional and spiritual. We made time for each other, not just in our schedules but in our hearts. We started dating again, trying to rediscover the excitement and curiosity we had early in our relationship. We explored new activities together, both inside and outside the bedroom, to break the monotony and reignite our physical connection.

We got creative. We experimented with new ideas and fantasies, communicating openly about what felt good and what didn't. This open line of communication helped us to reconnect not just sexually but also emotionally, reinforcing our bond and trust in each other.

Recognizing that our differing libidos could easily create tension, we approached our sexual relationship with an openness to exploration and creativity. Instead of seeing our mismatched desires as an insurmountable barrier, we viewed it as an opportunity for growth. We began to trust in the unique rhythms of our individual needs, finding ways to meet in the middle without pressure or guilt. Introducing new ideas and activities, we sought a playful harmony that could accommodate the ebb and flow of our desires. We treated our times of stress and fatigue not as excuses but as elements to work around, prioritizing rest and self-care so that when we came together, it was with energy and presence.

Amidst this renaissance of exploration, we reinforced a profound truth: our spirituality was not the enemy of our sexuality. In the sacred space of our marriage, they coexisted beautifully, each enhancing and deepening the experience of the other. We embraced the idea that our shared spirituality could infuse our sexual connection with an even greater sense of meaning and intimacy. We reminded ourselves that our union was more than just physical; it was a dance of the spirit, mind, and body, one that could thrive amidst life's demands if nurtured with intention, respect, and an enduring commitment to grow together.

And through it all, we kept reminding each other, our love life is worth fighting for. Each effort, each small change, reinforced the belief that we could return not just to normalcy, but to a vibrant, fulfilling sexual relationship.

Gradually, the silence and distance gave way to laughter, playfulness, and a renewed intimacy. We learned that marriage doesn’t have to dim with time; it can grow brighter, fueled by love, effort, and mutual respect. Our love life was no longer routine, it was revitalized, reflecting the depth and complexity of our life-long commitment to each other.

He Says:

Listen, brothers, there's no shame in saying your sex drive isn't always "on."
Stress messes with everything: your mind, your mood, your body.
And for me, when I feel pressure in life, it's hard to be fully present physically.

But here's what I learned: intimacy starts in safety.
When I felt safe to be honest with my wife, without feeling like I was disappointing her, it opened the door for reconnection.

Here's what helped us:

We stopped pretending. I shared when I felt disconnected, and she listened without judgment.

We focused on emotional intimacy first. Sometimes, a deep conversation unlocked what a romantic playlist couldn't.

We tried new things, together. We talked about our desires, our curiosities, and our boundaries. That vulnerability made us closer.

1 Corinthians 7:3 says, "The husband should fulfill his marital duty to his wife, and likewise the wife to her husband." But that "duty" isn't pressure, it's privilege. A chance to minister to one another through love, touch, and presence.

Our sex life isn't perfect, but it's alive. And better yet, it's ours.

She Says:

It used to frustrate me.
I had the desire.
The drive.
The need.

I had spent years doing the deep, painful, necessary work of healing, walking through the trauma of childhood sexual abuse, forgiving the betrayal of adultery in my first marriage, and surrendering the fear that intimacy would always be *wounded* for me. So, when I finally entered this marriage, **healed, whole, and holy, I was ready.**

Not just to love. But to *enjoy*. To *explore*. To *fully show up*.
But what I didn't expect was that, sometimes, my passion would be met with *pause*.
There were seasons when I was the one initiating everything. Sending the flirty text. Dropping the hints. Wearing the cute robe. And instead of meeting me with fire, I was met with **silence or subtle retreat**.

I took it personally.
"Is he not into me anymore?"
"Am I coming on too strong?"
"After everything I've overcome, am I still… too much?"

But in prayer, God gently interrupted that spiral.
He whispered to my heart:
"He's not rejecting you, he's retreating to protect you from what he can't yet articulate."
He wasn't pulling away *from me*, he was pulling back to survive. Stress. Fatigue. Inner weight. Instead of blaming him, I chose to *bless* our intimacy by doing what I had never been able to do before: **stay open. Stay tender. Stay whole.**

Because now, I had something I didn't have before, **clarity without shame. Desire without damage. A body and heart that had been through fire but refused to shrink.**

Here's what helped us spice things up without guilt or games:
I asked him what made him feel relaxed, not just turned on. I knew that passion started way before the bedroom. He stated to me, that our marriage has taught him it started with *peace.* With feeling seen. With not needing to perform or pretend. So we stopped trying to "schedule sex" and started building atmospheres where connection could breathe.

We made a "spice list." Yep, an actual list. Fun, flirty, spicy things we wanted to try. No pressure. No judgment. Just *permission* to explore the fullness of what God made for us, together. And baby… let's just say God knew what He was doing when He created married intimacy. Holy doesn't mean boring. Sacred doesn't mean stale.

I stopped tying my worth to his desire. His fatigue wasn't a reflection of my femininity. And my boldness wasn't a threat to his masculinity. When I stopped seeing his pause as rejection, he stopped seeing my passion as pressure. And in that safety, we found fire.

The verse that wraps it all up for me is **Song of Solomon 7:11–12**:
"Come, my beloved, let us go to the countryside… and there I will give you my love."
Translation?
Sometimes intimacy needs a *change of scenery*, physically, emotionally, spiritually.
Sometimes it's a weekend away.
Sometimes it's an open conversation.
Sometimes it's just holding each other in the stillness until your hearts find their rhythm again.

To every wife whose fire burns bright:
You are not too much.
You are not aggressive. You are *alive.*
And your desire is not a problem, it's a *gift.*

To every couple trying to reconnect:
Don't give up.
You may just need to *shift*, not shut down.
You may need to rediscover, not retreat.
Because when healed hearts meet in holy love, **intimacy becomes worship**.

A Heartfelt Message on Healing & Intimacy After Trauma
From My Heart to Yours

To the man or woman who has survived what never should've happened…

To the soul who knows what it feels like to flinch at touch, freeze at closeness, or carry the weight of shame that was never yours to begin with...

I see you. I am you. And I want you to know, you are not broken.

You are not too damaged to be loved.
You are not too guarded to be pursued.
And you are *absolutely* not disqualified from passion, pleasure, or partnership in the intimacy of marriage.

I know what it's like to carry the memory of hands that were not gentle. To wrestle with confusion between desire and fear. To want closeness but feel triggered by the very thing your spirit longs for.
But I also know what it's like to heal.
Slowly. Tenderly. Faithfully.

God can restore what trauma tried to steal.
He can rewire the way your body responds.
He can renew the way your mind thinks.

And He can send someone, a spouse, a partner, a safe place, who doesn't just want your body, but *wants to honor your heart.*
In my own journey, I had to relearn that intimacy is not something to *survive*, it's something to *share.* It is not just physical, it's sacred. And it is not about performance, it's about *presence.*

Your healing may not look like anyone else's. Some days you may feel open. Other days, unsure. Give yourself grace. Let your partner in. Let God guide the process. Because the same God who created your body with beauty and sensitivity is the One who knows how to restore it with safety and joy.

And when you finally experience intimacy that doesn't come with fear, but with trust… it's not just satisfying, it's *holy.*

To every survivor:
You are not your past.
You are not what they did.
You are not unworthy of love or pleasure or connection.
You are healing. You are growing. You are worthy of joy.

And when your heart is ready, *so is heaven*, to help you feel safe, seen, and beautifully desired again.

We Say:

Let's Talk About It: Bedroom Reset Conversation Guide

Step 1: Pray for Openness & Joy
Before the conversation, hold hands and pray together:

"Lord, thank You for the gift of intimacy. Help us to speak with truth, listen with love, and grow in joy. Let this time bring laughter, closeness, and trust, not pressure. Restore our rhythm and renew our passion. Amen."

Step 2: Talk About What's Working (and What's Not)
Each partner takes turns answering:

- "Lately, I've felt most connected to you when…"
- "One thing I still enjoy about our intimate life is…"
- "One thing I miss or would like to try again is…"
- "Something that's been affecting my desire (emotionally, physically, spiritually) is…"

Tip: Be curious, not critical. This isn't a blame session, it's a reset moment.

Step 3: Explore What "Spicing Things Up" Means to You
Each of you completes this phrase:

- "I've always wondered what it would be like if we…"
- Now rate the following ideas as a couple:

Idea	*[] Yes*	*[] Maybe*	*[] Not for us*
▪ Plan a weekend away (even local)			
▪ Use music, candles, or lighting to set the mood			
▪ Share romantic or flirty texts during the day			
▪ Have a "surprise me" date night			
▪ Read a Song of Solomon devotional together			
▪ Try new touch (massage oils, playful intimacy, etc.)			
▪ Take turns planning intimacy nights			
▪ Write a love letter or "fantasy note"			
▪ Have a "no-pressure" cuddle and talk night			

Revisit this list monthly! You'll be surprised how comfort and curiosity evolve with time and trust.

Step 4: Decide on One Action to Try This Week

Choose one low-pressure, joy-filled act of connection this week. Examples:

- "Let's have a no-kids, no-phones evening on Friday."
- "Let's trade flirty notes for 3 days and see where it leads."
- "Let's pray together and end with a long hug, every night."
- "Let's schedule intimacy instead of hoping for the right moment."

Scriptures to Meditate On Together

- **Proverbs 5:18–19** – "May your fountain be blessed, and may you rejoice in the wife of your youth…"

- **1 Corinthians 7:5** – "Do not deprive one another… that Satan may not tempt you."
- **Song of Solomon 1:2** – "Let him kiss me with the kisses of his mouth, for your love is more delightful than wine."

Affirmation Exchange

Before you close the conversation, take turns completing this:

- "I still desire you because…"
- "One thing you do that still makes me feel wanted is…"
- "I'm grateful that you're willing to grow with me in this area because…"

Closing Declaration (Say Together):

"Our intimacy is not behind us, it's in front of us. We will love with intention, touch with trust, and pursue each other without shame. God is in our bedroom, our emotions, and our future. And this part of our marriage is still holy, and still beautiful.

The Spice List: Reignite, Rediscover, Reconnect

"Let him kiss me with the kisses of his mouth, for your love is more delightful than wine." – Song of Solomon 1:2

How to Use:

- Each spouse completes the list separately (or together if preferred).
- Mark items as:
    - ✓ *Yes, let's try it!*
    - **?** *Maybe, let's talk about it.*
    - **✕** *Not for me.*
- Revisit every few months to check in, laugh, and grow!

Warm-Up: Connection Starters

Activity	✓	**?**	**✕**
Candle-lit dinner with no phones	☐	☐	☐
Flirty text messages throughout the day	☐	☐	☐
Sharing one thing you love about each other (daily)	☐	☐	☐
Couple's bubble bath or shower	☐	☐	☐
Holding hands during prayer	☐	☐	☐
Five-minute forehead-to-forehead breathing exercise	☐	☐	☐

Physical & Playful

Activity	✓	**?**	**✕**
Flirty role-play or pet names	☐	☐	☐
Massage exchange with oils or candles	☐	☐	☐
"No talking" kiss session for 5 minutes	☐	☐	☐
Trying a new room in the house (hello, couch!)	☐	☐	☐
Exploring lingerie (or themed outfits)	☐	☐	☐
Creating a romantic playlist and slow dancing to it	☐	☐	☐

Spicy but Sacred

Activity	✓	?	✗
Reading Song of Solomon aloud, seductively	☐	☐	☐
Whispering fantasies in a "no-judgment" zone	☐	☐	☐
Eye contact challenge: stare silently for 2 minutes	☐	☐	☐
Sensual scavenger hunt (you set the clues)	☐	☐	☐
Wearing blindfolds for sensation exploration	☐	☐	☐
Scheduling an intimacy weekend with no obligations	☐	☐	☐

Our "Yes, Let's Try It!" List:

Write down your mutual green-lights here and post it somewhere private as your intimacy invitation list.

1.
2.
3.
4.
5.

Final Reflection:

- What surprised you about each other's responses?
- What new spark did this list stir up?
- Are there any deeper conversations or prayers you want to have as a result?

Closing Prayer:

Lord, thank You for creating passion within the covenant of marriage.

Help us explore one another with joy, curiosity, and compassion.
Remove shame, fear, or insecurity, and replace it with trust, laughter, and holy fire.
Let our intimacy glorify You as we rediscover the beauty of our union, mind, body, and spirit.
In Jesus' name, amen.

Chapter Twenty-Three:

"SAY WHAT YOU NEED - WITHOUT FEAR OR SHAME"

Question:

How can I express my needs and desires effectively in my relationship?

Our Story:

She's always been clear. Confident. Centered. Self-aware. If she needed something, whether it was a hug, space, affirmation, or a moment of stillness, she spoke it. Kindly. Clearly. Unapologetically.

And I respected that about her. But I didn't know how to mirror it. Because I was the opposite. I was conditioned to *be strong.* To meet the needs of others before even acknowledging my own. I was always the supporter. The provider. The protector. Not because I didn't have needs, but because I had *never learned how to identify them without guilt.*

I don't recall anyone before my wife asking, "How are you really doing?" and then waiting until I gave an answer besides okay or fine.

I didn't know how to ask that of myself.
I knew how to lead. I knew how to serve.
But I didn't know how to say, *"I need comfort."*
Or *"I feel empty."*
Or *"I need help too."*

And in every relationship before this one, I never had the space, or the language, to explore it.
But she refused to let that silence become our norm.

The shift didn't happen by accident.
It happened through her **intentional, unwavering commitment** to *not just love me, but to see me.* To *hold space* for the man I was, while nurturing the man I was still becoming.

She didn't just wait for me to open up, she gently invited me there.
Again and again.
Through deep conversations.

Through small check-ins.
Through consistent grace.

She didn't push. She *pursued, with patience.*
With phrases that became healing refrains:
"It's not weak to speak up."
"I'm your partner, not just your provider."
"You're allowed to have needs, too."

And slowly, something shifted in me.
I started to look inward, at the parts of myself I had locked away.
I started asking myself what I needed, not just physically, but emotionally, spiritually, and relationally.
I started realizing that I didn't have to choose between strength and vulnerability, **they could coexist.**

Now?
Our connection is deeper.
Our communication is richer.
And our intimacy is no longer one-sided, it's mutual, layered, *honest.*
Because two whole people, who are willing to speak truth in love, will *always* build something that lasts.

I thank God for her, for the woman who didn't try to fix me…
but who *faithfully stayed present* long enough for me to find the version of myself I had never met before.

He Says:

As "our story" stated, for a long time, I thought my role in the relationship was simple: show up, provide, protect, serve.

But expressing my needs? That felt… unfamiliar.
Almost selfish.
Almost like I was putting pressure on her, or asking for more than I deserved.

But here's what I learned:

Silence doesn't protect your relationship, it slowly drains it.

When I stayed quiet, I built resentment. I wore invisible masks. I ran on empty, hoping she would just "notice" that I needed encouragement, rest, or intimacy.

Eventually, God convicted me:
"You're not a robot. You're a man, with a heart, emotions, and needs that matter too."

And her love? It gave me the space to be real.

Here's what helped:

I started naming emotions. "I'm not okay today." "I feel overlooked." "I could use your support tonight."

We made room for mutual needs. My "provider" role didn't replace my humanity.

I learned that asking doesn't mean demanding. It means inviting your partner into your world.

Scripture reminded me that even Jesus asked for help. In the garden, He said, "Could you not watch with me one hour?" (Matthew 26:40)

Even the Savior of the world needed companionship and support. So, do I. And, brothers, so do you.

She Says:

I entered our marriage with the mindset of being able to say what I needed. Not because I'm demanding. Not because I'm controlling. But because I've always believed that healthy communication is the *bridge* to emotional safety.

But early on, I realized, **he didn't think he had the same permission.** He had spent so much of his life serving others, fixing problems, holding people up, that *he didn't know how to acknowledge his own weight, let alone ask someone else to carry it with him.*

Thus, I made a decision. Not just to wait for him to find his voice. But to *lovingly help him uncover it.* I didn't want to just love the **man of God**. I wanted to love the **man**, the one behind the ministry.
The one who didn't always have the words.
The one who learned to survive by staying silent.
The one who was still healing in places he never had room to explore.
It took time.
It took *trust.*
It took consistency.
But I kept showing up, not to force answers, but to invite intimacy.

I didn't wait for him to speak up on his own, because I knew he wouldn't. Not because he didn't care. But because **he had been conditioned not to consider his own needs at all.**

I started asking, gently, intentionally, without pressure:
"What do you need from me this week?"
"Is there something you've been carrying that you haven't had space to release?"
"What would feel like love to you right now?"

And when the answers didn't come easily, I didn't shut down or take it personally.
I stayed.
I softened.
I *covered him in patience and prayer* until trust gave him permission to speak.

You see, when we got married, I already knew he was *more* than a protector or provider.
I never reduced him to the role of "strong man" or "spiritual leader."
I knew he was layered. Thoughtful. Tender.
I knew he had brilliance that hadn't been spoken into yet, and depths that hadn't been drawn out.
What he didn't know was that he didn't know it.
And that's where love stepped in.
Not to fix him.
But to hold space for his *becoming.*

And over time, I watched him start to reach for words he'd never used. He didn't just talk about tasks, he talked about tenderness. He didn't just carry weight, he started naming what it cost him to hold it. He began to speak, not from a place of performance, but from the *truth of who he was learning to be.* And in those moments, I didn't see less of the man I married, I saw *more.*
More depth.
More clarity.
More freedom.
Because real love doesn't just wait to be understood, it patiently teaches someone how to understand *themselves.*

Here's what I want other women to know: You might be the better communicator. You might be more emotionally aware. But don't let that turn into frustration. Let it become your *invitation* to lead in love, without control, but with compassion.

Don't just express, encourage expression. Ask the deeper questions. Wait for the real answers. Because *needs are not weaknesses.* They are **invitations to deeper understanding.**

The Bible says in **Ephesians 4:15**: *"Speak the truth in love…"*
That includes saying:
"I need you."
"I'm overwhelmed."
"I want to feel close again."

And it absolutely includes creating space for your partner to say the same. **Needs don't ruin connection.** Unspoken needs do.

For every wife who sees potential in her husband but senses emotional distance:
Don't rush. Invite.
Don't assume. Ask.
Don't give up. Hold space.

To every couple learning how to go beyond surface-level conversations:
Speak up. Slow down. Stay curious.
Because the right question, asked with the right heart, can unlock healing that silence tried to bury.

We Say:

Needs & Desires Expression Toolkit

Step 1: Pray for Openness & Understanding
"Lord, give us hearts that listen and mouths that speak with love. Help us share our needs clearly, receive them humbly, and respond with compassion. May we build a relationship where both of us feel heard, honored, and whole."

Step 2: Expressing Needs Clearly , "I Need..." Prompts
Take turns completing any of the following prompts. Speak honestly and gently. These aren't accusations, they're invitations for deeper care and connection.

"Right now, I need more..."

- ➤ [ ] Quality time
- ➤ [ ] Encouragement
- ➤ [ ] Affection or touch
- ➤ [ ] Words of affirmation
- ➤ [ ] Alone time
- ➤ [ ] Help with responsibilities
- ➤ [ ] Intimacy
- ➤ [ ] Prayer or spiritual support
- ➤ [ ] Something else: ____________

"This week, I would feel loved if you could…"

➤ ____

"One thing I've been holding in, but want to say, is…"

➤ ____

Step 3: Listening With Intent , "What I Hear You Needing..."
Now reflect back what you heard your partner say using soft affirmation:

- "What I hear you needing is…"
- "Thank you for sharing that, I didn't realize it was that important to you."
- "How can I love you better in that area this week?"

Pro Tip: Avoid solving. Just validate and clarify before responding.

Step 4: Create a "Care Map" Together
Pick 3 emotional or spiritual needs each of you have right now. Then list one way your partner can support or meet that need in the coming week.

Need	Support Action
(e.g., Encouragement)	Text me 1 uplifting word per day this week
(e.g., Intimacy)	Plan one intentional cuddle session with no distractions
(e.g., Clarity)	Sit down and do a calendar review together

Step 5: Establish a Monthly "Heart Check-In"
Put a 30-minute "talk and tea" (or coffee) time on the calendar once a month. Ask:

- What's been fulfilling me emotionally lately?
- What's been draining me?
- Is there a new need I haven't shared?
- How can we be more present for each other right now?

Bonus Tip: Bring your favorite snack, blanket, playlist, or sit in a relaxed setting, make the conversation feel like connection, not correction.

Scriptures to Meditate On

- **James 1:19** – "Be quick to listen, slow to speak, and slow to become angry."
- **Ephesians 4:2** – "Be completely humble and gentle; be patient, bearing with one another in love."
- **Galatians 6:2** – "Carry each other's burdens…"

Closing Declaration (Say Together)

"We are not afraid to speak truth in love. We honor each other's needs without guilt or pressure. We are safe, strong, and growing closer through honesty and grace. Our voices matter. Our hearts are heard. And we are still choosing each other, every day."

Chapter Twenty-Four:

"CLOSE, BUT NOT CONNECTED"

Question:

What can we do if our relationship is experiencing a lack of emotional intimacy?

Our Story:

We've sat next to each other on the couch, scrolling on our phones, sharing space but not connection. We've shared meals where the food was hot but the silence between us was cold. We've crawled into bed exhausted, offering a tired "Good night" instead of conversation, touch, or closeness.

We weren't angry.
We weren't in conflict.
There were no loud arguments or unresolved fights.
But we were *disconnected.*

And what made it harder was, we didn't see it right away.
Because disconnection doesn't always arrive with drama.
Sometimes it just *settles in* through busy days, long to-do lists, ministry demands, and the daily grind of managing everything *but each other.*
It was like our emotional intimacy got crowded out, not by big problems, but by small habits of neglect.

We started to feel it in subtle ways.
The way we stopped checking in.
The way we missed each other's sighs.
The way our "How was your day?" became robotic, and our answers became surface-level.

And one day, we looked at each other, and we *felt it.*
The space.
The stillness.
The ache for something deeper.
That's when we remembered a truth we both knew, but had to relearn:
Emotional intimacy is not built on convenience, it's built on intentionality.

It's more than talking.
It's more than being in the same room.
It's being safe enough to be vulnerable.
It's *choosing* to lean in, not just go along.
It's the moment you look across the table and feel seen.
It's knowing your thoughts matter, your fears matter, your unspoken sighs matter.
It's knowing someone is still reaching for *your heart*, even when life is loud and your schedules are full.

Here's what we learned, and what we want others to know:
You don't lose intimacy overnight.
And you don't rebuild it overnight either.
But you can *always* begin again.
You can turn the TV off and hold hands in silence.
You can set the phones down and say, "How are you *really* doing?"
You can sit on opposite sides of the couch and still find your way back to the *middle*.

When you make the choice to be emotionally present, even in small ways, God meets you there.
He breathes fresh grace into quiet places.
And He teaches you how to love each other all over again, with softness, curiosity, and depth.

He Says:

I didn't even realize we were drifting, until I looked over and saw her smile at her phone more than she smiled at me.

We weren't fighting. We were functioning.
But functioning without feeling is a slow emotional death.

That's when it hit me:

Emotional intimacy is built in small moments. Not just deep talks, but random check-ins, compliments, or asking "How are you really?"

I had to be vulnerable first. Instead of waiting for her to "open up," I needed to lead with my own heart.

I stopped trying to fix her feelings, and just started sitting with them even when her truth made me uncomfortable.

Proverbs 20:5 says, "The purposes of a person's heart are deep waters, but one who has insight draws them out." That's what emotional intimacy is, drawing each other out with gentleness, not force.

If you're feeling distant, brother, don't wait until it gets worse.
Start small. Show up. Ask questions. Pray with her. Sit beside her without distraction.

Closeness can be chosen again, today.

She Says:

You can be in love… and still feel lonely.

That's the hard truth I've had to share with some women in ministry, and even with myself during dry seasons.

We weren't disconnected in life, we were disconnected in soul space. And I started missing "us."

Not the calendar, the responsibilities, the work, but the soulful conversations, the vulnerability, the warmth.

To find our way back to each other we started with, "I miss us." We said it out loud. "I miss you." "I miss us." That honesty opened the door to reconnection. Rebuilding emotional intimacy begins with honesty. When we openly expressed our feelings, we created a pathway for reconnection. Saying "I miss us" acknowledged the distance that had grown between us and invited a conversation about our shared longing for closeness. This simple yet powerful statement broke down barriers and opened the door to vulnerability. By admitting "I miss you" and "I miss us," we validated each other's emotions and set the stage for healing. This honesty was the first step in rebuilding the emotional bridge that connected us, allowing us to move forward with a renewed sense of understanding and commitment.

We created emotional touchpoints again. We didn't start with grand gestures. We started with small, sacred moments that said, *"I see you, and I still choose you."* We began rebuilding emotional intimacy one intentional touchpoint at a time, simple, but powerful ways to *reopen the door to each other's hearts.*
Morning prayers. Not long or elaborate, just a moment to pause, hold hands, and invite God into our day. Sometimes it was just: "God,

cover us. Keep us connected. Let love lead today." It reminded us that even before the world demanded anything from us, we belonged to each other, and to Him.

Eye contact at dinner. No phones. No distractions. Just the steady, grounding presence of looking into each other's eyes and saying, *"You still have my attention."* It wasn't about the food, it was about presence. That quiet gaze said more than words: "I'm still here. I still want us." The table became more than a place to eat, it became a place to reconnect.

Reading out loud to one another. Whether it was Scripture, a devotional, a line from a book, or something funny we saw during the day, this act invited us back into shared conversation. It softened the atmosphere. It sparked laughter. It opened new dialogues. And in a world full of noise, *we chose each other's voice as sacred background music.*

Sharing reels and videos. Yes, even social media became a touchpoint. Funny reels. Silly dances. Memes that made us laugh. Or videos that made one of us say, *"This reminded me of you."* It wasn't just entertainment, it was *emotional shorthand.* It meant, *"I thought of you today. I still enjoy the things that make you smile."*

These emotional touchpoints weren't flashy. But they became holy ground. Because intimacy doesn't just live in the big moments, it's nurtured in the *daily return.* The slow, steady rhythms of, *"I see you. I care. I'm choosing you, again."*

We gave each other grace. We didn't blame each other, we reminded each other that we were still choosing to grow. Grace allowed us to acknowledge our imperfections and embrace the process of healing together. It meant forgiving each other for past mistakes and focusing on the present moment. By giving each other grace, we created a safe space where we could be vulnerable and honest without fear of judgment.

Emotional intimacy requires both presence and permission. Presence to stay even when it's quiet. Permission to be seen even when you don't have it all together.

Scripture that kept me grounded? Psalm 139:1–2 – "You have searched me, Lord, and you know me… you perceive my thoughts from afar."

That's what I craved, and that's what we started rebuilding.

To the couple quietly drifting? Don't give up.
Say what you need. Start soft. Stay kind. And trust that God can reconnect what time, stress, or silence has tried to separate.
Emotional and spiritual intimacy is not just the foundation of a strong relationship but its very lifeblood.

We Say:

Rebuilding Emotional Intimacy Challenge
(7 Days of Heart Connection)

Before You Begin: Set the Tone with Prayer
"Lord, help us slow down, open our hearts, and rediscover the emotional bond You placed between us. Teach us to be present, gentle, and honest. Restore our connection, not just in routine, but in the soul-deep intimacy that makes love lasting and whole."

Daily Challenge Schedule
Each day includes a theme, a connection prompt, and a scripture anchor. You'll need 15–30 minutes, no phones, and open hearts.

Day 1: "I Miss Us"
Prompt: Take turns sharing when you last felt most connected emotionally.
Scripture: "Two are better than one… if either of them falls, one can help the other up." – Ecclesiastes 4:9–10

Day 2: "I See You"
Prompt: Name 3 things you've noticed your partner doing lately (big or small) that you appreciate.
Scripture: "Be devoted to one another in love. Honor one another above yourselves." – Romans 12:10

Day 3: "No Fixing, Just Feeling"
Prompt: Share a recent emotion (joy, sadness, frustration, fear) and let your partner just listen, no fixing, no advice, just presence.
Scripture: "Rejoice with those who rejoice; mourn with those who mourn." – Romans 12:15

Day 4: "Hold Me Here"

Prompt: Sit or lay close, hold hands, and share what emotional closeness looks like to you right now. Be honest about what's missing or what's meaningful.
Scripture: "Draw near to God, and He will draw near to you." – James 4:8

Day 5: "Laugh with Me"
Prompt: Watch a funny clip, reminisce on a favorite memory, or do something light and playful together.
Scripture: "A cheerful heart is good medicine." – Proverbs 17:22

Day 6: "Pray Over My Heart"
Prompt: Pray aloud over your partner's heart, ask what they're carrying emotionally, and speak peace and encouragement.
Scripture: "Carry each other's burdens, and in this way you will fulfill the law of Christ." – Galatians 6:2

Day 7: "Still Us"
Prompt: End the week by sharing:

- What moment this week made you feel closest?
- What's one way you'd like to stay emotionally connected moving forward?

Scripture: "I found the one my heart loves." – Song of Solomon 3:4

Bonus Tips for Success

- Be gentle. This challenge is not for correction, it's for connection.
- Listen to understand, not defend.
- Physical touch (even holding hands or sitting close) deepens emotional connection.
- Keep notes or a journal if one of you processes better through writing.

Closing Declaration (Say Together)

"We are still growing. Still learning. Still choosing emotional intimacy over silence or survival. Our connection is worth protecting, restoring, and enjoying, together."

Chapter Twenty-Five:

"AFTER THE BREAK, IS THERE A WAY BACK?"

Question:

How can a relationship recover from infidelity?

Our Story:

Infidelity never showed up in our marriage, but we both knew its sting before we found each other. In our previous relationships, we had both lived through the hollow ache of betrayal. The unsteady breath when secrets came to light. The gut-punch of realizing that love alone doesn't always protect you from someone else's choices.

We had loved deeply… and been disappointed just as deeply. There were days we questioned ourselves. Days we tried to make sense of shattered promises. And nights we wept in silence, wondering if we could ever trust again. Infidelity didn't just break our hearts, it reshaped our understanding of intimacy, honesty, and covenant.

Even after forgiveness, the wounds lingered like echoes.
And while **God did heal those wounds**, they left behind something permanent, not bitterness, but *wisdom*. Wisdom about what love really requires when everything safe and familiar has been torn apart.

Then, as God would have it, our journey didn't stop with our own healing. He sent us couples, beautiful, broken, confused, ashamed, angry, weeping couples, who were navigating the aftermath of infidelity. Some wanted to fight for their marriage. Others weren't sure where to begin.

Some sat on our couch, barely able to make eye contact. Some reached out with trembling voices and guarded hearts. Some were betrayed. Some were the betrayers. And many didn't even know if their marriage had a heartbeat left to save.

But what they all shared was this:
They were standing in the wreckage, wondering if resurrection was still possible.
And over the years, here's what we've come to understand:

Infidelity isn't always the end of a relationship. But it is always the end of what that relationship *used to be.* If healing is going to happen, **something new has to be born**.

The old foundation, shattered by secrecy, sin, or silence, can't be rebuilt the same way.
Instead, healing demands a *holy reconstruction*:

- Truth without deflection.
- Repentance without excuses.
- Grace without denial.
- Humility without ego.
- And a willingness to do the painful, patient work of building *again.*

Not rebuilding back to what was, but building forward into what can be.
A relationship that is *truthful, transparent, tested, and tender.*

We've watched some couples do the work, and witness a rebirth of trust, respect, and passion they never thought possible.

We've also walked with others whose marriages didn't survive the breach, but whose *individual souls* still found healing.
Both outcomes required grace.
Both outcomes honored truth.

And both reminded us that **God is not only a restorer, He is a revealer.** He reveals what's been hidden, yes. But He also reveals the parts of us that we didn't know could rise again from brokenness.

To the couple navigating the aftermath of infidelity:
You're not alone.
You're not beyond redemption.
And you don't have to decide everything today.
But if you choose to heal, **know that healing is holy work.**
It is sacred.

It is slow.
And it is *possible.*

If the two of you are willing to be brutally honest…
Willing to sit in discomfort without running…
Willing to pursue God even when trust is shattered…
Then yes, there *is* hope.

And sometimes, on the other side of heartbreak, you don't just find recovery. You find a relationship that's *rebuilt with fire, forged in faith, and anchored in grace.*

But we've also seen the other side.
We've sat with couples who loved God, tried counseling, prayed fervently, and still couldn't find a way back to each other.
We've walked beside spouses who offered forgiveness, but were met with continued betrayal.
We've watched trust crumble under the weight of repeated lies, emotional detachment, or the refusal to do the work.

And in those moments, we learned something just as sacred:
Not every marriage survives infidelity.
But *every person* can.

Because while God loves marriage, He also deeply loves *you.*
He is not glorified by you staying in something that destroys your spirit. He is not honored by you shrinking into silence, pretending to heal while bleeding internally.

Sometimes, walking away isn't giving up. It's *getting up*, and choosing healing even if it has to happen outside the covenant that was broken.

And for those who've had to grieve not just what happened, but what never got restored, please hear this:

You are not a failure.
You are not unlovable.
And your future is *not canceled* because your marriage didn't make it.
God still has plans for you.

Plans to heal, to restore, to rebuild your confidence, your joy, your trust in love again, even if it looks different than what you hoped.
You can move forward.
With wisdom.
With dignity.
And with peace.
Because **redemption isn't just about saving the marriage. It's about saving *you*.**

He Says:

As a man who has been on the betrayed side before, I can tell you, infidelity doesn't just hurt your heart. It shakes your identity.

You question your worth. Your discernment. Your whole sense of reality. And if you choose to stay? You've got to know this: recovery isn't quick, and it isn't one-sided.

When we counsel couples in this space, I always tell the one who committed the betrayal:

- You have to be fully transparent. No more hiding. No more vague answers.
- Don't rush your spouse's healing. Forgiveness doesn't mean instant trust.
- Let your changed behavior be louder than your promises.

And to the one who was hurt:

- It's okay to grieve. Feel all of it. But don't live there.
- Decide what you need to see to even begin rebuilding.
- Get wise, outside counsel. You need help to see clearly in the fog.

Biblically, we lean into 2 Corinthians 5:17 – "If anyone is in Christ, they are a new creation…" If both of you are willing to die to the old ways, God can build something new. But both people have to do the work.

Sometimes it's repairable. Sometimes it's not. But either way, you can heal. You can recover, even if the relationship doesn't.

She Says:

Infidelity doesn't just break trust, it breaks security.
Even years later, betrayal from a past relationship shaped the way I viewed closeness. I had to fight the voice in my head that whispered, "It will happen again."

So when we sit with couples who are walking through this pain, I come with empathy first. Because I've felt that ache. That swirl of anger, sadness, shame, and numbness all at once.

Here's what I always say when we counsel couples walking through the aftermath of infidelity:
Healing can happen, but not without truth and accountability.
You can't heal what you keep hiding.
You can't restore what you keep denying.
You don't heal by pretending it didn't happen.
You heal by *telling the truth, sitting in it, and then walking through it, with help, with humility, and with God.*

Man or Woman - if you're the one who was unfaithful, let me be direct:
An apology isn't a magic eraser.
You don't get to say, "I'm sorry" and expect your spouse to bounce back with full trust and open arms.
You must *become someone they feel safe with again.*
That means consistency. Transparency. Accountability.
That means sitting in their pain without defensiveness.
That means understanding that the healing timeline doesn't revolve around your comfort, it revolves around *their recovery.*

And again, man or woman, if you're the one who was hurt - let me speak directly to your heart:

You're not weak for being brokenhearted.
You're not bitter for having questions.
And you are not faithless for needing time to process.
It's okay to take your time.
It's okay to say, "I'm not ready."
It's okay to say, "I'm trying, but I still don't trust yet."

What's *not* okay is staying stuck without seeking God, growth, or guidance.
So be honest. Get support. Ask the hard questions.
But also check your heart for areas that need healing, too, not blame, but *honesty*.

And let me say this too, with gentleness and truth:
Not every marriage will make it through infidelity.
Some will be rebuilt, stronger, wiser, and more connected than before.
But others may end, and **that does not mean you failed.**
If someone continues to cheat…
If they continue to lie…
If they're not willing to change or walk the road of restoration…
You are not obligated to stay in brokenness just to prove your loyalty.
God honors covenant, yes.
But He never asks you to sacrifice your *dignity, sanity, or safety* in the name of keeping up appearances.

The verse I anchor myself in, whether walking with couples who are reconciling or with individuals finding peace after divorce, is **Psalm 34:18**: *"The Lord is close to the brokenhearted and saves those who are crushed in spirit."*
God doesn't rush your healing.
He doesn't shame your confusion.
He doesn't walk away when you're unsure if you can ever trust again.
He **holds you** through it.
He **carries you** when your strength gives out

And He restores, not just what you lost, but the *you* that got lost in the pain.

Beloved, take a breath.
Take your time.
And take your healing seriously.
Because whether the marriage survives or not, **you are still worthy of a whole, honest, joyful love**, starting with the one God is pouring back into *you*.

We Say:

What We Recommend to Couples After Infidelity:

Pause major decisions. Don't rush to stay or leave in the shock of discovery. Get quiet. Get counsel. Get perspective.

Seek therapy and spiritual covering, immediately. Not just as individuals, but as a couple if you choose to rebuild.

Set truth as the new foundation. No more secrets. No vague answers. Full honesty, even when it hurts.

Create a restoration plan. What does rebuilding trust look like for your marriage? What are the boundaries, expectations, timelines?

Be willing to release what cannot be repaired. If it ends, let it end in peace, not in bitterness.

Restoration or Release? Decision Framework

Start With a Centering Prayer (Together or Alone)

"God, we don't want to make this decision out of pain, pride, or fear. Help us see with clarity, feel with compassion, and respond in love. Whether we stay or separate, let healing be our goal and grace be our guide."

Step 1: Clarify What's Been Broken

Each partner should answer these questions honestly:

- ? What exactly was broken (trust, intimacy, identity, communication)?
- ? Has the full truth been shared, or are secrets still lingering?
- ? Has the betrayer acknowledged the damage without minimizing it?

? Has there been evidence of repentance, not just regret?

Note: If truth is still incomplete or repentance is performative, rebuilding cannot begin.

Step 2: Discern Willingness to Rebuild

Ask yourselves:

? Is both of us willing to do the deep, uncomfortable, long-term work of rebuilding?

? Are we willing to go to counseling, together and separately?

? Can we create and commit to clear boundaries that protect both people emotionally and spiritually?

? Can the betrayed spouse be honest about what they need, without fear of being told they're "too much" or "too emotional"?

If **both partners are not equally invested**, restoration becomes one-sided, and healing may stall or not occur.

Step 3: Set Rebuilding Expectations

Use this chart to clarify what is needed for trust to even begin to rebuild.

Rebuilding Element	Are We Doing This?
Total transparency (phones, passwords, time)	Y/ N
Individual counseling	Y/ N
Marriage counseling	Y/ N
Consistent spiritual covering	Y/ N
Grace and space to ask questions	Y/ N
Defined boundaries with people involved	Y/ N
Time-limited check-ins and progress reviews	Y/ N

Step 4: If Releasing the Relationship Becomes Necessary

Not every relationship survives betrayal, and that's not a spiritual failure.

If you choose release:

- Do it with honor, not hate.
- Involve a wise, spiritually grounded support system.
- Focus on healing, not blaming.
- Forgive, even if reconciliation isn't possible. Forgiveness is for freedom, not permission.

Matthew 19:8 reminds us that divorce was permitted because of hardness of heart, not because God wanted it, but because humans are imperfect. And even when release happens, God still restores.

Step 5: Ask the Holy Spirit for Peace

Both together and individually, sit quietly and ask:

- "Do I have peace to stay?"
- "Do I have peace to go?"
- "Is my heart open to healing, regardless of the outcome?"
- Wait. Listen. Write what you sense.

Scriptures for This Season of Discernment

- **Psalm 34:18** – "The Lord is close to the brokenhearted…"
- **2 Corinthians 5:17** – "If anyone is in Christ, they are a new creation…"
- **James 1:5** – "If any of you lacks wisdom, ask God…"
- **Isaiah 43:19** – "Behold, I am doing a new thing…"

Closing Declaration (Say Together If Rebuilding):

"We are choosing to rebuild, with truth, time, tenderness, and trust. We will not pretend. We will not rush. But we will move forward, with God's help, one day at a time."

Closing Declaration (Say Alone or Together If Releasing):

"We are choosing healing, peace, and release. We will not hate. We will not harm. We will let go, so that God can do something new in each of us."

Final Thoughts:

"Still Standing, Still Choosing, Still Becoming"
Real Love. Relevant Truth. Raw Grace

Final Thoughts from Bishop Jai and Dr. Ki,

If you've made it this far, first, thank you.
Thank you for reading.
Thank you for showing up for your healing.
Thank you for daring to lean in when it would've been easier to scroll past, shut down, or say, "That's not for me."

Whether you're **single and seeking**, **dating with intention**, **engaged and preparing**, or **married and maturing**, this book was written with *you* in mind.

It wasn't written from a mountaintop of perfection.
It was birthed from prayer, personal reflection, heartbreaks we've survived, grace we've received, and real conversations we've had with real people, just like you.

It's the story of two imperfect people, deeply in love with God and each other, saying: "Let's not pretend. Let's be real. Let's grow on purpose, love with clarity, and heal with intention."

We've walked with couples through wedding days and baby dedications. We've also sat with individuals crying through breakups, grieving betrayal, or wrestling with whether to stay or walk away.

And in every relationship, whether it was just forming or decades deep, we've learned this:

Love is not perfect. But it must be protected. Not just from outsiders, but from *assumptions*, *emotional drift*, *unspoken needs*, and *the quiet lies the enemy whispers when you feel alone*, even in the same room.

Relationships are not performances. They are processes. Whether you're dating, married, or healing from a breakup, growth happens in the tension, when honesty replaces hiding, and truth replaces pretending.

God is not absent from the hard parts.
He's in your journaling session.
He's in the "should I call or let it go?" moment.
He's in the couple's therapy room, the brave boundary conversation, the quiet surrender when love hasn't shown up yet, but you're still believing it will.

God doesn't just meet us at the altar, He walks with us in the aftermath even as we are continually being altered.

So, what now?
Now, we invite you to keep doing the work, whatever season you're in:

- If you're **single**: Keep becoming. Keep healing. Don't rush love. Prepare for it with wisdom.
- If you're **dating or engaged**: Keep asking the hard questions, building strong foundations, and choosing clarity over chemistry.
- If you're **married**: Keep praying, pursuing, prioritizing one another, and never stop learning how to love better.

Let this book be a reference, a reminder, and a resource. Come back to it. Talk through it. Share it with your friends, your small group, or your future spouse. Use it to grow forward.

A Final Word of Blessing:

May the Lord bless your relationship journey, wherever you are, with courage, joy, and truth. May your heart be guarded but not closed. May your words be seasoned with grace, and your ears attuned to God's whisper. May you pursue love that reflects heaven, steadfast, sanctified, and spirit-led. May you forgive yourself for past mistakes, give grace for present growth, and trust God with your future story. And when it gets hard, and it *will*, may you remember that real love is built, not just felt. That becoming is a process, and that you don't have to do it alone.
You are still standing.
Still choosing.
Still becoming, by grace, with truth, and for God's glory.

With love, truth, and raw grace,
The Two of Us
(Your Brother & Sister in Christ, Your Fellow Relationship Fighters)

Becoming Before Belonging: A Sacred Pause for Singles

Prayer of Recommitment for Singles

"Preparing for Real Love"

God, I come to You with a heart that is open, tender, and honest.
Thank You for walking with me through this journey, showing me what love looks like when it's sacred, not superficial.
I recommit myself to You first, trusting that You are shaping me for love that honors Your heart.
Where I've been wounded, bring healing.
Where I've settled, stir up vision.
Where I've questioned my worth, remind me I am chosen, cherished, and created for connection.
Teach me how to love without fear.
To speak truth with compassion.
To guard my heart without hardening it.
To wait well, live well, and grow deeply, even before love arrives.
And when the right relationship comes, let me walk into it whole, not hiding.
Let me recognize what is real.
Let me be bold enough to receive it.
Let me be wise enough to protect it.
Until then, I'm choosing faith.
I'm choosing healing.
I'm choosing me, becoming the person I'd want to marry, and becoming someone You can trust with the gift of covenant love.
In Jesus' name, Amen.

Personal Reflection: "My Real, Relevant, and Raw Journey"

Take a moment to pause and reflect on what you've learned through this book. Write as much as you'd like, you may return to this page later and add more as you grow.

What parts of the book made me feel most seen, understood, or challenged?

____

What areas of love, dating, or healing do I still need to bring to God?

____

Where have I grown in how I view relationships, marriage, or myself?

____

What am I praying for in a future partner? What am I becoming in the meantime?

____

One truth I'm carrying forward from this book is…

____

Real Talk Between Me and God: Journaling Prompts for Singles

God, here's what I'm learning about myself in love and life:

____

God, here's where I still feel vulnerable or unsure:

____

God, help me grow in the area of…

____

God, here's what I hope my future relationship will feel like:

____

God, prepare me to be a safe, whole, and joyful partner by…

____

Real Affirmations for Real Becoming

Speak these aloud or write them in a journal as daily affirmations:

- I am becoming who God created me to be, patient, whole, and rooted in love.
- I am not behind, I am being built.
- I do not chase love, I prepare to receive it.
- I trust God's timing, even when it tests me.
- I am worthy of real, respectful, joy-filled connection.
- I will not shrink to be chosen. I will grow to be ready.

Next Steps: Preparing with Purpose

- ✓ Revisit this book during new seasons of growth, highlight chapters that speak to where you are.
- ✓ Create your "Relationship Readiness Journal", capture your prayers, deal breakers, boundaries, and goals.
- ✓ Stay surrounded by wise counsel and spiritually grounded friendships.
- ✓ Pray for your future partner, but also pray for *you* to remain soft, strong, and surrendered.
- ✓ Mentor someone else. Tell your story. Let your journey prepare the way for someone else's healing.

Built to Last:
A Sacred Pause for Couples

Prayer of Recommitment (Together as a Couple)
"God, we come to You with open hearts, thankful for where we've been, and hopeful for where we're going. We recommit ourselves to one another. Not just with words, but with consistent love. Give us the courage to tell the truth, the grace to forgive, the strength to grow, and the humility to learn. Teach us to be lovers, listeners, protectors, and prayer warriors. Where we've been broken, bring healing. Where we've grown cold, reignite the flame. Where we've drifted, draw us back, not just to each other, but to You. Let our relationship reflect Your heart, Your patience, and Your redemption. We choose each other again. In Jesus' name, amen."

Couple's Reflection: "Our Real, Relevant, and Raw Journey"
Spend a moment writing and sharing together:

What parts of our relationship felt most seen or affirmed through this book?

____

Which question stretched us the most?

____

Where have we grown during this journey?

____

What's one area we want to keep working on together with God's help?

____

One truth we'll carry forward from this book is...

____

Individual Journal Prompts: "Real Talk Between Me and God"
You can each respond to these privately, then share together if you feel led.

God, here's what I'm learning about myself in relationships:

____

God, here's what I still struggle to say or show in love:

____

God, help me grow in the area of…

____

What I want my partner to know about me is…

____

I believe our relationship can become even stronger by…

____

Bonus: Real Affirmations for Real Love
Write or speak these over one another at the close of your journey:

For the Wife to Say:
"I see you. I value you. I still choose you. We've come far, and we'll go further. You're a safe place for my heart."

For the Husband to Say:
"I honor you. I need you. I still want you. You are my help, my joy, and my answered prayer. I'll keep choosing us."

Next Steps
Schedule a "relationship retreat day" once a year to revisit your answers and celebrate your growth.

Consider reading this again in a future season. Mark the chapters that meant the most.

Pray about mentoring another couple. Let your testimony give others hope.

About the Authors

Married since July 2011, Bishop James "Jai" Watson and Dr. Nikita "Ki" Garris-Watson are the heart and leadership behind Real, Relevant, and Raw: Real Talk, Sacred Insight. Their love story, marked by God's grace and relentless commitment, has become a living testimony of what it means to build, battle, and believe together. As ministry leaders, authors, and mentors, they have dedicated their lives to equipping couples with practical and spiritual tools to cultivate strong, purpose-filled relationships.

Together, they serve as the Senior Leaders of Words of Deliverance Worldwide Ministries (WODWM), a non-denominational, mobile ministry with a mission to "matter, not to be mega." Rooted in deliverance, transparency, and restoration, WODWM exists to build relationships that heal individuals and communities alike.

Bishop Jai Watson is a respected spiritual leader, philanthropist, and the CEO of Strong Man Ministries, where he stands on the frontlines of spiritual warfare for the healing of families, especially men. Known for his authenticity and compassion, Bishop Jai lives by the motto, "meeting people where they are so they may get to God." His ministry is grounded in the power of prayer, fasting, and practical application of God's Word. He brings over two decades of leadership experience from the commercial trucking industry, which he sacrificially left to serve closer to home and help restore broken lives. He is the visionary author of *Brewing Wit' Da Bishop: Prayer on Tap* and its powerful companion, *Prayer on Tap: The Workbook*. Known for his bold voice, prophetic insight, and relatable wit, Bishop Jai equips believers to cultivate a deeper, more intentional prayer life. Through these transformative resources, he invites readers to not only talk to God, but to *grow* with God, offering spiritual nourishment that's always "on tap."

Dr. Nikita "Ki" Garris-Watson, affectionately known as The Stiletto Preacher, is a survivor, strategist, and spirit-led trailblazer. As an Apostle, bestselling author, educator, and CEO of Dr. Ki Enterprises, she uses her own testimony of childhood and adult abuse to bring deliverance to both the neighborhood and the nations. Armed with a Bachelor's degree, two Master's degrees, a Doctorate of Ministry, and a fire for transformational impact, Dr. Ki operates at the intersection of faith, education, healing, and justice.

Through her teaching, speaking, and writing, including her bestselling books *Damaged But Destined: So What? Now What!* and *Damaged but Destined: The Deliverance Diary*, she proves that **pain can become purpose and brokenness can lead to breakthrough**. These works are not just inspirational, they are **instructional**, equipping readers with spiritual tools to confront their past, embrace their healing, and walk boldly in their divine assignment.

Her books have become healing guides, journaling companions, and altar calls in written form, sparking tears, deliverance, and transformation in living rooms, churches, and even hospital rooms. Her voice carries both **fire and compassion**, challenging readers to face what hurt them, while lifting them toward what God has for them. Dr. Ki doesn't just write from theory, she writes from **the trenches of testimony**, where trauma was met by truth, and shame was silenced by Scripture.

Whether she's speaking from the pulpit, leading a workshop, or signing books at an outreach event, her message remains the same: **You may have been damaged, but you are still destined. And your destiny deserves your full healing.**

Their lives are a reflection of the message they preach: that love, when rooted in God, can endure storms, inspire change, and lead to purpose-driven impact. As co-authors, Bishop Jai and Dr. Ki bring you into their world, complete with laughter, lessons, hard questions, and holy answers. They believe marriage is a ministry, and family is a sacred assignment.

They are the proud parents of four amazing, anointed children: Quinton, Steven, Kyra, and Sasha. While they work to impact the world, they are fiercely committed to protecting their greatest ministry, their home.

Together, their calling is clear: To be real, stay relevant, and embrace the raw, with grace, truth, and unwavering love.

Connect with the Watsons:

RealRelevantAndRaw@gmail.com

Bishop Jai
StrongManMinistries31@gmail.com
Facebook: StrongManMinistries_31
Instagram: StrongManMinistries_31
TikTok: StrongManMinistries_31
Twitter/X: StrongManMinistries_31

Dr. Ki
Facebook: IAmDrKi
Facebook: DrKiEnterprises
Instagram: IAmDrKi
TikTok: IAmDrKi
Twitter/X: IAmDrKi
Website: www.DrKi.org

Made in the USA
Middletown, DE
23 June 2025

77371761R10159